WINSTON CHURCHILL

Biography®

WINSTON CHURCHILL

James C. Humes

LONDON, NEW YORK, MUNICH,
MELBOURNE, and DELHI

DK PUBLISHING
Publisher Chuck Lang
Creative Director Tina Vaughan
Editorial Director Chuck Wills
Art Director Dirk Kaufman
Production Manager Chris Avgherinos
DTP Designer Milos Orlovic

First American Edition, 2003
2 4 6 8 10 9 7 5 3 1
Published in the United States
by DK Publishing, Inc.
375 Hudson Street
New York, New York 10014

produced by AVALON PUBLISHING GROUP, INC.
Project Editor Max Alexander
Senior Director, Editorial Will Balliett
Senior Director, Operations f-stop Fitzgerald
Photo Editor Tracy Armstead
Designer Lisa Vaughn
Assistant Editor Kristen Couse
Production Manager Mike Walters
Production Editor Simon Sullivan

A&E TELEVISION NETWORK
Director of Licensing Carrie Trimmer
Director Legal and Business Affairs Chey Blake
VP/GM Consumer Products & Merchandising Steve Ronson

A&E and Biography are trademarks of A&E Television Networks.
All Rights Reserved © 2003 AETN

Jacket design copyright © 2003 A&E Television Networks
and DK Publishing, Inc.
Text copyright © 2003 James C. Humes

Photo Credits—See page 152

DK Publishing, Inc. offers special discounts for bulk purchases for
sales promotions or premiums. Specific, large-quantity needs can
be met with special editions, including personalized covers,
excerpts of existing guides, and corporate imprints. For more
information, contact Special Markets Dept., DK Publishing, Inc.,
375 Hudson Street, New York, NY 10014 Fax: 212-689-5254.

Cataloging-in-Publication data is available from
the Library of Congress
ISBN 0-7894-9318-7

Reproduced by ColourScan, Singapore.
Printed and bound by R.R. Donnelley in the United States.

See our complete product line at
www.dk.com

Contents

Churchill: The English Bulldog

Soldier, Statesman
Winston Churchill (wearing the uniform of a Hussar) embraced the military traditions of the British Empire while encouraging the modernization of the armed forces.

In the midst of World War II, Winston Churchill visited his old school. The assembly hall of Harrow was jammed with students as well as many of their parents, who stood in the back to hear their Prime Minister. The headmaster, nervous at the challenge of presenting his renowned guest, tried to pack in his lengthy introduction the many accomplishments and honors of Churchill. Churchill acknowledged with a nod and delivered a simple commandment address, jabbing his finger toward the young men in his audience.

"Never, give in! Never give in. Never, never, never, never, never, never—in nothing great and small, large and petty. Never give in—except to convictions of honor and good sense."

That is the story of Sir Winston Churchill. He never gave in. He never gave up. He never gave up on his country. He never gave up on his principles. He never gave up on himself.

Churchill was clearly the man of the 20th century, as *Time* magazine called him half a century ago, and a recent poll agreed. On his 90th birthday he received a card from a young girl in Mexico City. The envelope was addressed to the Greatest Man in the World, with no other words of name or destination, yet it arrived.

The reasons for his greatness are manifold. His span of influence on the world stage is unparalleled in history. He served in the cabinets of two world wars. His service in Parliament bridged most of the 20th century, from 1900 to 1964. In 1900 he swore his oath to Queen Victoria, and in 1955 when he resigned the prime ministership, he was hosted at a dinner by Queen Elizabeth. As a subaltern, he rode in the last British cavalry charge in the Sudan in 1898. As prime minister in 1953, he made the decision for Britain to test the H-bomb.

He looms in history like an Old Testament prophet. He foretold both world wars as well as the Cold War, not to mention the atom bomb, the energy crisis, the eight-hour workday, and the creation of Israel. His gift of prognostication seemed almost supernatural. For example, he predicted precisely—three years before it happened in 1914—that Germany would invade France through Belgium, and that its advance would not be stopped until the 40th day at the Marne river. Edward R. Murrow said of him, "He is the only man in the annals of time to prophesy history, make history, and write about it."

Churchill was also a Renaissance man, possessing the wide genius of Leonardo DaVinci or Benjamin Franklin. As an author, he saw more works published than Hemingway, Faulkner, and Dickens put together, and he was honored with a Nobel Prize for Literature.

As a soldier, he braved gunfire on four continents, barely escaping death. As an artist, his works were exhibited in the Louvre. Picasso, who despised Churchill's politics, said "if he had stuck to oils, he would have reached first rank." As an inventor, he was "the father of the tank" and came up with the idea of mobile landing harbors for the Normandy beach. Besides his books and paintbrush, he found time in a busy parliamentary career to be a ranking polo player until his '50's, a licensed brick mason and a breeder of racehorses.

The most famous portrait photograph of the last century was the one taken of Churchill by Youssuf Karsh in Ottawa in December 1941. Just before Karsh snapped it, he snatched the cigar from Churchill's mouth. A disgruntled Prime Minister scowled, and that look of bulldog defiance was captured for posterity. Indeed, Churchill himself wrote: "The chin of the bulldog juts out so that he can bark and growl but never let go with his teeth."

"Never Give In"
Compromise was a rare action for Churchill. Here he strikes a typically defiant pose when heckled by Communists in Brussels, Belgium, in March 1949.

Youth
1874–1892

On December 3, 1874, the *Times* of London printed this birth notice: "On the 30th of November at Blenheim Palace, the Lady Randolph Churchill prematurely of a son."

From the day of his birth, Winston Churchill was in a hurry.

Jennie Churchill had intended to produce her firstborn in London, but destiny took over. A cradle in a palace—like a log cabin or a manger—was a more notable entry point than 48 Charles Street, London, his parents' first home.

Jennie may have contributed to Winston's premature birth by going for a bumpy carriage ride, followed by an evening of dancing at the St. Andrew's Ball at Blenheim Palace. Winston was born, at about seven months, in a coatroom off the ballroom. The wife of a lawyer at the ball had to rush back to her nearby home and fetch baby linens for the new boy.

If Jennie did right in arranging Winston's noble birth site, she got poor marks in bringing him up. In short, as Winston's own son later wrote, she was "neglectful" as a mother, preferring evenings out to time in the nursery. For Winston, his mother was like "The Evening Star, I loved her dearly—but at a distance"

His father was even more distant. Lord Randolph's neglect of his son bordered on cruelty and would shape his own son's role as a father. The opposite of a strict parent, Winston never insisted on discipline, and always indulged his children.

BLENHEIM PALACE

"My two greatest decisions," wrote Winston Churchill, "were made at Blenheim. I decided to be born and I decided to be married." Yet long before Winston's own birth in a coatroom of the Oxfordshire palace, Blenheim had stood as a symbol of British victory.

The palace was a gift from Queen Anne to Sir John Churchill, the first Duke of Marlborough (and direct ancestor of Winston), in gratitude for his conquest of Louis XIV's armies at the Battle of Blenheim in August 1704. Construction of the palace, designed by the architect Sir John Vanbrugh, began the following year.

Vanbrugh envisioned the 300-room palace as a monument to England's military triumph over France—and perhaps as England's own answer to Louis XIV's Versailles. Its ornate Baroque style recalls the

The parkland surrounding Blenheim Palace is featured in Sir Walter Scott's 1826 novel *Woodstock: Or, the Cavalier*. Perhaps Scott was inspired by the literary musings of Blenheim's designer, Sir John Vanbrugh. In 1697, before he became an architect, Vanbrugh wrote two novels: *The Relapse* and *The Provok'd Wife*.

facade of St. Peter's Basilica in Rome, and the gardens and watered terraces (laid out by landscape architect Capability Brown) add to the splendor.

Winston did not grow up at Blenheim; it was his grandfather's house, which his parents visited infrequently. But Blenheim did shape the boys' imagination and ambition. Today, Blenheim is owned by the present Duke of Marlborough and can be toured. Less than a mile from the palace, in a small graveyard in the town of Bladon, Winston Churchill lies under a simple headstone beside his parents and his wife.

Lord and Lady Randolph moved among the beautiful people who clustered around the raffish Prince of Wales, later King Edward VII. But in 1875, Lord Randolph made the Prince of Wales' blacklist. The Prince of Wales had been infuriated by Randolph's older brother, the Marquess of Blandford, who had stolen away his mistress.

The Countess of Aylesford, the lover of Edward, had left him to tryst with Lord Randolph's brother. So an irate Prince of Wales leaned on the countess's husband, the earl, to sue for a divorce and name the Marquess of Blandford as correspondent. With indiscreet, if impassioned, loyalty to his brother, Lord Randolph got word to Edward that if a divorce proceeding ever took place, he was going to make sure that the prince's love letters to Lady Aylesford would be leaked to the newspapers. Had that happened, the whole affair might have become the 19th-century version of the Charles-and-Diana tribulations. Edward's mother, Queen Victoria, would not have been amused.

The prince retaliated by letting it be known that he would not set foot in any household that entertained Lord and Lady Randolph. In a London that took its cue from the dashing prince, Randolph and Jennie became social pariahs. Invitations ceased. The high-society world was no longer hospitable—it was hostile.

Yet, as is so often the case, what at first seemed like an obstacle became a blessing. Lord Randolph's banishment from the parlors of London triggered his transformation from social dilettante to political maverick. With nothing to lose, he became Britain's most outspoken and passionate young politician. And Winston, who might otherwise have become a banker or a teacher, followed in his father's footsteps to the House of Commons.

Lord Randolph didn't change overnight. Immediately after the impasse with the prince, Lord Randolph's father, the Duke of Marlborough, deemed it best to take his two sons out of London, so he took the post of viceroy in Dublin, making his younger son, Randolph, his secretary. (In an Ireland still ruled by Britain, the viceroy was essentially the deputy king.)

Four years later, in 1879, the social chill had thawed enough for a return to London. Lord Randolph, by then eager to make himself a name to be reckoned with in society, entered politics with a reckless bravado and a gift for speaking that established him as a national personality.

His son, Winston, meanwhile, was having no such fun. From a child's point of view, it doesn't matter whether his mother goes out to work in a factory or to attend the opera or a ball. In any case, he is left alone. Winston's mother and her friends were like apparitions in feathered boas, flower-decked hats and perfumed handkerchiefs. They swept into the nursery on holidays and birthdays, bearing presents and blowing kisses before heading off to another event. His only constant

Distant Parents
Churchill's father Randolph (above) and mother Jennie (below) were focused on politics and London social life, not their two children.

WOOMY

Baby Winston was adored by his nanny, Mrs. Everest.

Just before Christmas in 1874, Lady Randolph engaged the services of Anne Everest as nanny for the month-old Winston. A childless widow in her early forties, Everest had served previously for another family. In Churchill's baby talk, *woman* became *woomy*, and that is what he called her the rest of his life. If young Winston figured little in his parents' attentions, Woomy would remain his champion and chief encourager. She was the first person he would see in the morning, and the one who kissed him good night.

Woomy was let go in 1891 when Winston was 17, but the lad protested to his mother, arguing that his brother Jack was still a young boy and needed her care. To bid her farewell, Winston sent her train fare to come see him at Harrow School. There they held hands and walked across the Common, despite the derision of his classmates.

When she died in 1895, Winston made the funeral arrangements and paid for the headstone. At Chartwell, Churchill's home in Kent, her picture rested on his nightstand, where it can still be seen today.

comfort was his beloved nanny Anne Everest, whom he called Woomy (for woman). But at age seven, Winston learned to his dismay he was being sent to boarding school. Now he wouldn't even have Woomy.

By contemporary standards, shipping a seven-year-old off to boarding school seems crushingly sad. In fairness, however, 19th-century society was not nearly so child-centered as today. And from a purely physical standpoint, much worse fates awaited poor children, who were often made to work in dangerous factories at that age. Still, Winston's parents seemed unusually disinterested in both Winston and his brother Jack, who was born in 1880. In later years Churchill often wrote of his disappointing childhood, but only in matter-of-fact terms. He was of a generation that rarely acknowledged personal feelings, much less aired them in public. Thus we will never know how his lonely boyhood truly affected him. Clearly though, his success as an adult was a testament to the resilience of the human spirit.

The headmaster of St. George's School, where he was sent, was the Rev. H. W. Sneyd-Kinnersley. His Dickensian name matched the nature of a school that combined Uriah Heep obsequiousness to parents with a Bill Sykes sadism to its pupils.

When Churchill received poor grades, Sneyd-Kinnersley would take him to his room, strip him, and flog him until his bottom was a mass of blood. A visitor to the school once noticed a little red-haired youth running around in dizzying circles for hours. "Who is that?" she asked. "Why that's young Churchill," the headmaster replied. "It is the only way we can keep him quiet."

The punishments did not diminish the Churchill spirit. He sneaked into the headmaster's study and found the principal's prized straw hat and stomped it to pieces.

Churchill's miserable career at St. George's was predicted by his first Latin lesson. He was ordered to memorize the declension of the word *mensa*, meaning "table." Winston was puzzled at the vocative case.

"It means," said the master, "O table! You would use it in addressing a table."

"But I never do," replied the confused Winston.

"If you continue to be impertinent, you will be punished and punished very severely," the master reprimanded him.

Winston's parents may not have been concerned about their child, but Woomy was. When the nanny noticed the black and blue marks on his fair white skin when he returned for a weekend visit, he was switched to a school in Brighton at her insistence.

At Brighton, a seaside resort south of London, the loneliness, if not the lashes, continued. He wrote his mother after he was returned to Brighton from spring vacation: "You must be very happy without me ... it must be heaven on earth."

At Brighton, Winston once read that his father had come to deliver a political speech in the town. "I cannot think why you did not come to see me while you were in Brighton," he wrote. "I was very disappointed, but I suppose you were too busy to come."

The only thing he enjoyed at Brighton were the school plays, where his natural acting skills were rewarded with leading roles. *Robin Hood* was his favorite, and he played the title role. But the audience of parents gave him the warmest reception in a play titled *The Heir at Law.* He brought the house down with his continued misreading of the line "I will send my carriage." Instead of "carriage" he said "carrot," which, since it was the color of his flaming hair, triggered gales of laughter. Alas, neither of his parents attended any of his school performances.

Contrary to his enthusiasm for the stage, his work in class was below average. In fact, his first year at Brighton ended with him at the very bottom of his form. Yet his grades improved enough for acceptance into Harrow, a "public" school in northwest greater London. There, too, he did not win any prizes for his academics or comportment. After a host of infractions, Churchill was called to the headmaster's office. Dr. Welldon raised his six-foot frame from his chair and stared down at his insubordinate pupil. With his hands folded behind his back, Welldon intoned, "Young man, I have grave reasons to be displeased with your conduct."

Winston looked up and replied with equal solemnity, "And likewise, I have grave reasons to be displeased with you."

As Churchill later wrote of his

Apt Pupil?
Young Winston was described by his headmaster at St. George's School as "a regular pickle." It was not meant as a compliment: a foe of tyranny at an early age, Winston rebelled against boarding-school discipline.

LADY RANDOLPH

"The wine of life was in her veins," Churchill wrote about his mother, Lady Churchill. She was born Jeannette Jerome in Brooklyn in 1854, the daughter of Leonard Jerome, an American financier, whose ancestors had fought the British in the Revolutionary War. Like his famous grandson, Leonard was a horse-racing enthusiast. He helped found the American Jockey Club; the Jerome Park Racetrack in the Bronx (and nearby Jerome Avenue) were named after him.

Jennie met Lord Randolph on a yacht in August 1873 off the Isle of Wight. She had previously gone boating with Napoleon III, and she was being courted simultaneously by two French dukes.

Lord Randolph, too, was smitten at first sight. They married hastily at the French embassy in Paris in April 1874, and Winston was born seven months later.

Lady Randolph with her two sons, Jack (left) and Winston, in 1885. Winston adored his younger brother, who fought at Gallipoli in World War I and died in 1947. His daughter Clarissa married Anthony Eden, Churchill's foreign secretary and successor as prime minister.

According to some biographies, her affairs ran to the hundreds. She chose as her lovers the rich, bright, and powerful—including the future king Edward VII. He wrote love letters to her in French, signing A.E. (Albert Edward).

After Lord Randolph's death in 1895, Jennie performed charitable work and then became an author and playwright. She remarried, but her second husband left her for the famous actress Mrs. Patrick Campbell—who had starred in a play written by Lady Randolph. She married a third time to a man younger than Winston. After falling down stairs and developing gangrene in her leg, she died in 1921 at age 67.

experience at Harrow: "This intolerable school makes a somber grey patch upon the chart of my journey. It was an unending spell of worries…and of toil uncheered by fruition; a time of discomfort and purposeless monotony."

The only bright patch on that bleak canvas was his discovery of the beauty of the English language. Winston loved English as much as he detested Latin and Greek. His failures in the "dead" languages made him repeat a year. But his command of English grammar was such that he was asked to take over the English class and teach his fellow classmates. From a teacher he learned diagram sentences, using colors for the various parts of speech—blue for the subject, red for the verb, yellow for an adjective, orange for an adverb, and green for a preposition.

As Churchill later wrote of his Harrow experience: "Thus, I got in my bones the essential structure of the ordinary English sentence, which is a noble thing." He added, not totally in jest: "Naturally I am biased in favor of boys learning English. I would make them all learn English, and then I would let the clever ones learn Latin as an honor and Greek as a treat. But the only thing I would whip them for is not knowing English. I would whip them hard for that . . ."

> "No boy or girl should ever be disheartened by lack of success in their youth but should diligently and faithfully continue to persevere and make up for lost time."
>
> WINSTON CHURCHILL

At Harrow, the resourceful Winston found a way to make his proficiency in English compensate for his deficiency in Latin. He struck a deal with a young Latin whiz who couldn't put his mind to writing the assigned English compositions. In return for this linguist's translations, Winston ghosted his essays. One of these struck the fancy of the headmaster, who called the Latin scholar into his study to expand upon his interesting conclusions. Afterward the shaken youth told Winston he'd like the conclusions a bit less dazzling. It was not to be the last time people found Churchill's brilliance unsettling.

Under the pseudonym Junius Junior, Winston wrote for the school paper, the *Harrovian.* Just as he would later take ministers to task for their inadequacies in meeting various contingencies, he attacked the condition of the school pool, workshop, and gym. The headmaster, who suspected the identity of the anonymous writer was none other than Lord Randolph's son, gave him an indirect warning:

CONTEMPORARIES

Notable world figures born in the same year as Churchill include:

• Herbert Hoover, U.S. president
• Chaim Weitzmann, first president of Israel
• Guglielmo Marconi, Italian physicist
• G. K. Chesterton, British author
• Robert Frost, U.S. poet
• Ernest Shackleton, British polar explorer
• Gertrude Stein, U.S. poet
• Arnold Schönberg, German composer

Churchill, incidentally, outlived them all.

"My boy, I have observed certain articles which have recently appeared in the *Harrovian* of a character not calculated to increase the respect of the boys for the constituted authorities of the school. As the *Harrovian* is anonymous, I shall not dream of inquiring who wrote these articles, but if any more of the same sort appear, it might become my painful duty to whip you."

Unbowed, Winston persuaded his editor to print one more broadside:

"All these things that I have enumerated serve to suggest that there is 'something rotten in the State of Denmark.' I have merely stated facts—it is not for me to offer explanation of them. To you, sirs, as directors of public opinion, it belongs to bare the weakness."

Winston's feel for the language was soon matched by a love of history, the second course in which he quickly excelled. At Harrow, they still display the paper he wrote when he sketched a "World War I" scenario of machine guns, trench warfare, and armies drawn mostly from civilians instead of career soldiers.

That the descendant of John Churchill, Duke of Marlborough, was fascinated by the military arts is not surprising. The boy's favorite childhood escape had been playing with his toy soldier collection. He could pretend he was the duke, organizing his regiments to beat the French. His maneuvering of miniature soldiers far surpassed those of the usual childhood game. He organized entire wars, not just battles. Under Winston's command, massive battalions of soldiers were mobilized. He launched peas and pebbles against enemy fortifications, sent cavalries charging to the rescue, and destroyed bridges and roads.

Once, in the midst of a battlefield deployment, Winston's father entered his room. It was one of the first real conversations Lord Randolph had with his son. "Winston," he intoned, "would you like to be a soldier?"

"Yes, Papa," he said. Later, Lord Randolph told his wife, "Winston is too naughty for the clergy, too stupid for the law. So it's the military for him."

Strange as it may seem, those careers were about the only choices for upper-class Britons of the time. A career in business was unthinkable; aristocrats did not involve themselves in "trade." (By the end of the 19th century, banking was emerging as an acceptable business career. Still, some of the leading firms in Britain were headed by Jewish families, like the Rothschilds—friends of Lord Randolph. To old-line aristocrats, the Jewish influence underscored that banking was merely a more refined form of trade.)

Instead of going into business, aristocrats who went to "public schools" like Eton, Harrow, or Winchester qualified for Oxford or Cambridge (if they were smart), where they would earn degrees to preach, teach, or practice law. If they were not so clever, they became

Harrow Days

Harrow School (opposite page, in 1964) was founded in 1571 and counts among its alumni the poet Byron and Spencer Perceval, the only British prime minister to be assassinated (in 1812). At Harrow, Churchill loved fencing but hated most of his schoolwork.

LORD RANDOLPH

Churchill's father Randolph was born the son of the Seventh Duke of Marlborough. He was not the eldest son, however, so the ducal mantle did not pass on to Winston's line of the family. After schooling at Eton and Oxford, Lord Randolph readily found his place in public life—initially as a Member of Parliament from Woodstock, a small borough that included the family's ancestral home of Blenheim Palace. Lord Randolph dazzled Parliament with his oratory and wit. He rose in the Conservative Party for his rhetorical skill in demolishing William Gladstone, the Liberal prime minister, and in 1886 he became the youngest chancellor of the Exchequer in history. (The chancellor is in charge of Britain's finances and is the second most powerful person in government.)

Randolph's meteoric rise was short-lived, however. In 1890 he fell from favor after challenging his own party's prime minister, Lord Salisbury, on what Churchill regarded as an excessive military budget. (As a leader of so-called "Tory Democracy," Lord Randolph favored more domestic spending.)

His rash move may have been spurred by the early effects of syphilis, which he probably contracted after a liaison in Paris. Medical care of the time had no cure for venereal disease, and Randolph slowly went mad before his death in 1895.

Lord Randolph believed aristocrats had a duty to serve their country.

career soldiers—unless they inherited some landed estate. Then their life would be that of a country squire.

To a boy like Winston, soldiering had its romantic appeal. His head was filled with fantasies of sword-fighting French officers in Marlborough's army, or dueling with one of Cromwell's Roundheads in the service of King Charles. It was no wonder that fencing became his top sport at Harrow. In March 1882, he begged his father to watch him compete at the Public School Fencing Championship. But Lord Randolph preferred the competition of horses at Ascot. "It is the races I must go to," he told the boy. The horse he bet on at Ascot did not win, though his son placed first in fencing that day.

Team sports like rugby, field hockey, and cricket held no interest for Churchill. He relished the spotlight of the solitary challenge in sports like fencing or swimming. When he left Harrow, he held the school's best time in swimming freestyle races.

For the same reasons, he disdained choral singing in favor of acting—as long as he was given a lead role. He did so in Shakespeare's *Henry V* and *Merchant of Venice*. Able to memorize verse easily, he tried out for all the poetry recitals—which were competitive events like spelling bees, where the goal was to recite long passages perfectly from memory. In his first year, he came in third reciting a thousand-line piece from Shakespeare's *Richard III*. He wrote his father: "I was rather astonished, as I beat some twenty boys who were much older than I." His father did not reply.

The next year he tried again. This time it was a thousand lines from Macaulay's poem *The Lays of Ancient Rome*. The day before the event, he learned that the required number was actually twelve hundred lines, so he stayed up most of the night in the dormitory bathroom to memorize the additional words. Some of the lines were:

> Then none were for a party
> Then all were for the state
> Then the great man helped the poor
> And the poor man loved the great
> The lands were fairly portioned
> And the Huns were fairly sold
> The Britons were like brothers
> In the brave days of old.

The rolls of Harrow for that year note, "W.S. Churchill P." (The "P." stands for prize.) It was one of Churchill's two scholastic honors at Harrow. Again, his parents did not attend Speech Day to see him win the prize.

Two other subjects at Harrow bear mentioning for the way they would shape the adult in the boy. The first was drawing, at which Winston excelled. In a letter to his mother, he wrote excitedly about his sketches of "little landscapes & bridges & those sort of things." Years later, landscape painting became one of his great avocations.

The second subject was German, which he described to his mother in one very Germanic word: "Ugh." But he didn't give up. "I hope to be able to "Sprechen ze Deutche"[*sic*] one of these days," he wrote.

Churchill never did learn to speak German, but he left Harrow speaking English better than many of his teachers. The actor in the boy was shaping the orator in the man.

The Play's the Thing
Churchill's favorite Shakespeare play was *Henry V* (below, the title page for the 1608 edition). During World War II, he asked Laurence Olivier to produce and star in a film of the play, to boost morale. The film won a special Academy Award.

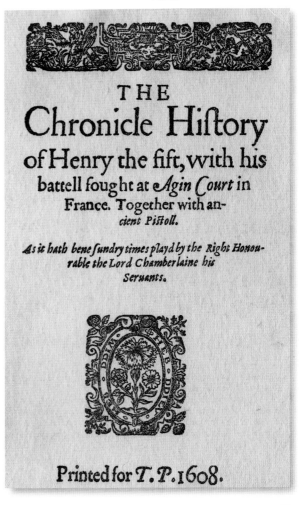

THE
Chronicle History
of Henry the fift, with his battell fought at *Agin Court* in France. Together with ancient *Piſtoll*.

As it hath bene ſundry times playd by the Right Honourable the Lord Chamberlaine his Seruants.

Printed for *T.P.* 1608.

Soldier
1892–1899

Churchill may have been slated for a soldier's career, but he almost didn't make it into the Royal Military Academy at Sandhurst. In his last term at Harrow, his old nanny, Mrs. Everest, wrote to him that he had to buckle down not only "to please his Lordship and your Mama but to disappoint some of your relations who prophesy a future of profligacy for you."

At Harrow, Churchill had enrolled in the army class and had also joined the school cadet force, where he mastered the firing of the Martini-Henry rifle, which was used by the army. If, however, he did not pass his army exams, he would probably not get into Sandhurst (the British equivalent of West Point) and become a clerk in some London bank. Lord Rothschild had promised Jennie to find a slot for him.

Twice Churchill failed his army exam. If his third examination paper fell below a score of sixty, he would be forever barred from qualifying for the Royal Military Academy.

In studying for the exam, Churchill decided to concentrate on the geography question that amounted to one-fifth of the total grade. He snipped maps of the British dominions out of an atlas and dumped them into a top hat, figuring he had time to study only one. Putting his hand over his eyes, he shuffled them around and pulled out one. It was New Zealand. He traced and retraced the natural features of the North and South Islands, memorizing every mountain and bay of what was then the British colony.

On examination day, the sergeant major who was giving the exam wrote out on the blackboard: "Question #1 (20 points): Draw a map of New Zealand."

As Churchill told it later: "It was like breaking the bank at Monte Carlo. I drew both islands, put in the key cities and river. Then I added the parks, the libraries, and even the tram lines. I got the full twenty points!"

For Churchill, Sandhurst was more than a military school; it was the start of manhood. It was time to grow up. In 1893, he could see his father, Lord Randolph, "dying by inches," as former Prime Minister Rosebery said. About that time, Churchill had his only constructive conversation with his father. His father apologized for his moody tempers and asked his son not to judge him too harshly and to understand that he really meant well and wanted the best for his son. Lord Randolph talked about his political career and about Winston's future as a soldier.

It was now make or break for Winston. His ranking at Sandhurst would determine the future of any military career. The result was that at Sandhurst, instead of finishing up at the bottom of the class as he had at Harrow, he came close to the top. At Harrow he mastered the secret of Napoleon's success: *"L'art de fixer les objets sans être fatigué."* ("The art of concentration without tiring.") It was one of the few French phrases he ever quoted regularly, even if in his atrocious accent. Churchill later instructed his son Randolph that he must develop the ability to throw himself into an unfamiliar field or subject and master its essentials. It is the mark of any great trial lawyer or orator. Later Randolph wrote of his father: "He had to fight every inch of his road through life; nothing came easily to him, not even oratory or writing, in which he later was to excel. To achieve success, he had to develop that intense power of concentration." So if out of his studies at Sandhurst Churchill never became a general, it made him a generalist—the prerequisite of any great leader.

In his eighteen-month stay at Sandhurst, Churchill applied himself as he never had at Harrow. He mastered courses like tactics, fortification, topography, and military law, finishing twentieth in a class of 130. If this was not the brilliance of a Douglas MacArthur or a Robert E. Lee, who finished at the top of their West Point classes, it was better than Omar Bradley or Dwight Eisenhower, who were respectively 44th and 61st in a class of 160.

At Sandhurst, Churchill also began to assemble his first library. He ordered Prince

A Capable Cadet

Churchill (left, with Sandhurst classmates) excelled at military school—partly because, he wrote, he was "no longer handicapped by Latin, French and mathematics." But he was dismal on the athletic field—"cursed," he observed, "by so feeble a body."

SANDHURST

Sandhurst Royal Military Academy, located 33 miles southwest of London, is an unfrivolous and stern collection of functional buildings where Britain's military leaders have trained since 1802. The class buildings and dormitories are ringed by lakes and forests that open onto bleak and silent moors.

Among Churchill's fellow students were the future kings of Spain, Siam (Thailand), and Ethiopia. They were graded on their ability in making land mines, digging trenches, blowing up bridges, and following contour

Sandhurst (above) was grim—but not as bad as West Point, wrote Churchill, who was shocked to learn that U.S. Army cadets were not allowed to smoke or carry money.

maps. Unlike West Point, Sandhurst does not award academic degrees. It grants only military commissions, and studies last just eighteen months, not four years.

Students at Sandhurst live a spartan regimen and obey strict rules. The toughest for Churchill might have been "Shouting in college buildings is strictly forbidden."

Kraft's *Letters on Infantry,* and Sir Henry James Sumner Maine's *Infantry Fire Tactics.*

He also began to collect a set of friends, which he never really had at Harrow. It was because of these fellow cadets that Churchill delivered his first public speech in 1894.

It was not what one might call a maiden address. In fact, it was an exhortation in support of unvirginal pursuits. Their spartan regimen, from reveille at 6:00 A.M. to lights out at 11:00 P.M., made the cadets eager to let off steam on their few weekends off campus. The destination was always London, where a favorite hangout was the Empire Theatre—a music hall in a neighborhood frequented by prostitutes. During breaks between the variety skits, Sandhurst cadets and other young men stepped outside and bantered with the women who strolled by. The solicitation had become notorious enough that the Women's Entertainment Protection League mounted a campaign to clean up the place. This "bluenose" lobby erected canvas partitions

along the sidewalk to prevent streetwalkers from catching the eyes of young blades drinking at the theatre's bar. The cadets enlisted Churchill's help to resist the moral crackdown.

One night Churchill and some like-minded officers bought tickets to a performance at the Empire. During intermission, Churchill roared: "Charge the barricades!" The canvas partitions on the sidewalk were quickly ripped down. Then Churchill mounted the stage of the theatre and condemned "the prowling prudes" who would deny Londoners their civil liberties. His speech closed with the words: "Gentlemen, you have seen us pull down the barricades. See that you pull down those who are responsible for them at the coming election!"

It was an auspicious performance that left Churchill swelling with pride, but his celebratory mood was short-lived. That same weekend, while staying with his mother, Churchill learned of his father's venereal disease and approaching death. Though Churchill never commented on the cause of his father's disease, it must have shaken him. Chastity is not considered one of the cardinal virtues of military life. Yet despite his trips to the Empire with his Sandhurst friends, Churchill himself was never known to associate with the prostitutes. Later, in India, Cuba, North Africa, and the Boer War, Churchill never acquired the reputation of a "sport" among his companions. In fact, some biographers suggest he was a virgin when he married. After watching syphilis destroy his father, Churchill might well have feared venereal disease enough to abstain from casual sex.

Winston received his commission at Sandhurst in December 1894. His father died in January. Six months later, Woomy died. These deaths released him from the last ties with his childhood. Subaltern Churchill entered manhood at age twenty.

But in 1895, the newly-turned-out Hussar cavalryman found himself all dressed up with no place to go. There was no field on which to make a move. Hardly a cloud darkened the horizon of the British Empire. About the only war taking place in the world was in Cuba, which was fighting for independence from Spain. To Cuba he would go, but he first stopped off in New York City to visit Bourke Cockran, his mother's former lover and cousin by marriage. He was captivated by Cockran, a Democratic congressman, and his week in New York was the beginning of a mentorship that would last nearly thirty years.

For Churchill, Bourke Cockran was the father he had wanted Lord Randolph to be. Like his own father, Cockran was a brilliant politician. As Randolph Churchill had won a First at Oxford, so Cockran had excelled at

Cavalryman
Churchill (at the time of his commission as a lieutenant in the Fourth Hussars) had wanted to be a cavalryman since childhood. In order for Churchill to be released from the Cambridge Rifles and assigned to the Hussars, his mother appealed to the Duke of Cambridge.

Trinity College in Dublin. Also like Lord Randolph, Cockran defied his own party. Lord Randolph attacked Prime Minister Lord Salisbury in 1886, and Cockran campaigned for Republican William McKinley against William Jennings Bryan in 1896. Cockran also supported Republican Theodore Roosevelt in 1904 and again in 1912, when Roosevelt ran unsuccessfully for his own Progressive Party.

But unlike Churchill's father, Cockran was intimate and engaging. He welcomed young Churchill into his circle, and drew him into long and animated discussions about classic literature. "Bourke's conversation exceeded anything I have ever heard," Churchill later wrote.

Cockran talked to Winston as an equal, sharing his own political philosophies and plans, as well as his secrets in speech preparation and delivery. Once he took Winston to one of his trials. Afterward, he advised him never to clutter his argument with lots of points. "To present a case, you have to pick the strongest argument on your side and concentrate on that—build and mount that to conclusion." It was advice that Churchill never forgot.

From New York, Churchill sailed to Cuba. There he had secured a position as an observer with the Spanish army, as well as a correspondent's contract with the London *Daily Graphic* to write a column a day for £5. Though Cuba gave him his first taste of gunfire, his start as a journalist was more significant. For an untrained eye, young Churchill was prescient. He sensed the paradox that would describe every revolution in the following century. As he put it: "I liked the rebellion but not the rebels." He thought the cause right but the conspirators behind it rotten. They would sell out the people they pretended to serve.

In Churchill's mind, the Spanish colonial government was corrupt and merited overthrow. Yet he condemned the terrorist actions of the rebels—including the burning of houses and farms where civilians were killed. Although he admired José Martí, the Cuban poet and revolutionary leader, Churchill found most of his fellow rebels unsavory.

During Churchill's sojourn in Cuba, he experienced a memorable twenty-first birthday. On November 30, 1895, a bullet fired by a rebel soldier

BOURKE COCKRAN

Bourke Cockran was a model for 20th-century politicians Churchill and FDR.

Churchill's friend, the eight-term New York congressman Bourke Cockran, has been largely forgotten by time. But during the early 20th century he was a giant of the American political scene. Born in Sligo, Ireland, in 1854 (the same year as Churchill's mother), Cockran was a trial lawyer who mastered the art of jury persuasion. Cockran's flowing white mane of hair, ruddy cheeks and silvery baritone voice were all part of his appeal. He claimed to be a distant relative of the British orator Edmund Burke, and he was a second cousin to Oscar Wilde. In New York, he worked his way up through the Tammany Hall political machine and gained fame as a fire-breathing speaker. Three times he was picked to keynote the Democratic Party's national convention. Cockran helped convince Franklin Roosevelt to return to politics after being stricken by polio in 1921. He died in 1923.

BIRTH OF THE MOVIES

Many film scholars trace the birth of modern cinema to December 28, 1895—the day Louis Lumière first projected films in front of a paying audience in Paris. One of the short films thrilled viewers with a shot of a train roaring into a station, seemingly right at the audience. Churchill, whose daughter Sarah became a film actress, loved movies, which he often screened at Chequers (country home of the British prime minister) during World War II.

Foreign Correspondent
Churchill (seen as a 25-year-old correspondent in the Boer War) gained early fame as a journalist and author. His reports from from Cuba for London's *Daily Graphic*, and from South Africa and the Sudan for the *Morning Post*, paved his way as a chief chronicler of his era.

passed clean through his hat. It was an anointment rite of manhood, and Churchill celebrated that evening by puffing his first cigar.

A taste for Havana cigars was one of two lifetime habits that Churchill picked up in Cuba. The second was his discovery of the Spanish siesta, taken midday with clothes removed, which he found added at least three productive hours to the day.

When Churchill returned to England, he learned that his unit of Fourth Hussars had been called to India. Most of his fellow officers welcomed this assignment to the subcontinent in the heyday of the Raj, where colonial life spelled one continuous round of polo and parties. But Churchill wanted a war where he could win fame. He had told his mother, "I want to seek adventure, find glory, and write about it." Money from books would be the means to afford a life in politics.

There wasn't much adventure in Bangalore, India, a central southern city perched 3,000 feet above sea level. The activities consisted of mounted drills during the morning and polo in the afternoons. Churchill loved polo, but was soon bored talking about it. He grew weary of the bungalow chatter dwelling only on flesh, be it equine or feminine.

Instead, no doubt inspired by his conversations with Cockran, Churchill decided to educate himself. Because his courses at Sandhurst were entirely technical, Churchill had no higher learning in the liberal arts. So he established what he called a "university of one." As both teacher and student, and he gave himself assignments for the week. During three or four hours in the torrid midday, when his fellow officers played cards, Winston read what he would have studied at Oxford or Cambridge. Then on Sunday he administered his own tests—making himself write essay answers to his own questions—on his readings in history, economics, and philosophy.

Churchill yearned for the erudition of his father and Cockran. He sent urgent letters to his mother, requesting piles of books. The first to arrive was Edward Gibbon's *Decline and Fall of the Roman Empire*, which his mother said had been his father's favorite. Then came Thomas Macaulay's various histories of England. Winston gave himself assignments to read twenty pages of Gibbon and fifty of Macaulay every day. He found he could absorb more if he interspersed his readings among several authors.

Macaulay and Gibbon became the co-stars of Churchill's expanding bookcase, and the two historians influenced him tremendously. "I affected a combination of the style of Macaulay and Gibbon," Churchill later wrote, "the staccato antitheses of the former and the rolling sentence and genitival endings of the latter."

Macaulay was acidic and aphoristic. His style was punchy, almost conversational, with much alliteration. When Churchill later wrote, "A fanatic is one who won't change his mind or change the subject," he sounded like Macaulay. The same with "All wisdom is not new wisdom."

But if Churchill was amused by the wit of Macaulay, he was more impressed by the weight of Gibbon, whose stately prose is what we hear when

Churchill described FDR: "That great man whom destiny has marked for the climax of human fortune." Churchill also picked up the tricolon of the Gibbon sentence, as in his famous World War II line: "In war, resolution; in defeat, defiance; in victory, magnanimity."

What Churchill particularly admired was the balance of the Gibbonian sentence, in which an aura of impartiality masked a devastating opinion. Thus Gibbon would concede the virtues of an emperor with "although" or "while" in the subordinate clause, and then excoriate him in the main part of the sentence. ("While Theodore indulged the Goths in the enjoyment of rude liberty, he servilely copied the institutions and even the abuses of the political system.")

After historians Gibbon and Macaulay, Churchill followed with philosophers—first the ancient Plato and Aristotle, then the modern Darwin and Hegel. At the same time, he asked his mother to send him copies, beginning with his birth date of 1874, of the *Annual Register* (the parliamentary equivalent of the *Congressional Record*). As an intellectual challenge, he would not read the debates until he had first read the bill in question. Then he wrote out his own speech before reading the debated pros and cons.

The fact was that Winston didn't want to be a soldier. He wanted to be a politician, like his father. Churchill now had so many thoughts in his head that he was ready to explode. He needed an audience. On his first home leave from India, he dropped into the Conservative Party's office. To his amazement, he was asked to speak at a local Tory function. He wrote later: "It appears there were hundreds of indoor meetings and outdoor fêtes of bazaars and rallies—all of which were claimant for speakers. I surveyed this prospect with the eye of an urchin looking through a pastry cook's window. Finally, we selected Bath as the scene of my maiden effort."

Churchill wrote and rewrote the draft in his mother's home at Cumberland Place. In front of the mirror, he rehearsed. He decided to open with the lines of a popular song:

Every eyelid closes
All the world reposes
Lazily, lazily, drowsily, drowsily
In the noonday sun.

For a transition, he segued: "Parliament is dull today but by no means idle." He then gave attention to some items in the Conservative Party's program. This gave

THE NOVELIST

Churchill (in 1904) tried his hand at just about every form of writing except drama.

One of Churchill's lesser-known literary efforts is a novel he wrote in 1898 called *Savrola: A Tale of the Revolution.* The book, which he completed in several weeks, takes nothing away from Dickens or Kipling—but it remains remarkable as a work of prophecy.

The story is set in Laurania, a fictional state somewhere in the Balkans. The leader of Laurania is Molara, an insensitive autocrat who can't communicate with his people but nonetheless has secured a beautiful wife named Lucile. Savrola is the leader of the opposition; he wants to remove Molara from office—but like Hamlet, he can't bring himself to act.

Molara is clearly modeled after Churchill's uncommunicative father, and his radiant wife Lucile is, of course, Lady Randolph. Elements of Savrola suggest Churchill himself—especially his characterization as a talented speaker.

But most interesting is a fourth character—a German corporal named Kreutze, one of Savrola's followers who eventually takes control. Kreutze is a foaming maniac who screams himself into command as the country's new socialist messiah. It's one thing to model characters after your parents. It's another to predict the rise of Hitler.

Incidentally, in the book, Molara is killed, and Savrola escapes into exile with Lucile.

him the chance for some choice sallies against "radicals who will never be satisfied, and Liberals, always liberal with other people's money." The radicals, he wrote, "reminded me of the man who on being told ventilation was a good thing, smashed every window in his house and died of rheumatic fever." On the other hand, Conservative policy was "a look-before-you-leap policy." His keynote line followed: "The British working man has more to hope from the rising tide of 'Tory Democracy' [his father's old phrase] than from the dried-up drain pipe of radicals."

Then he sent an advance copy of his speech with a press release to the London newspapers. This ploy, which had never been tried before even by members of Parliament, indicated Churchill's ingenuity and initiative. As a result, the *Daily Mail* sent a reporter to Bath to cover the son of the late Lord Randolph. On the train to Bath, Churchill recognized the veteran columnist and made him listen to a dress rehearsal of the speech.

The actual address was received enthusiastically. The Primrose League audience was an organization his father had founded in honor of Disraeli. (The primrose was Disraeli's favorite flower.) Afterward, G. W. Stevens wrote: "He may or may not possess the qualities of a great general . . . but he has the qualities which might make him . . . a great popular leader, a great journalist, or a founder of a great advertising business."

But one speech did not satisfy his craving for action. While home on leave, Winston saw a newspaper headline that caught his eye. Fighting had broken out on the northwest frontier of India, in what is now Afghanistan. General Bindon Blood was putting down the uprising. Blood, whom Churchill had met through his mother, had promised Winston that he would take him along if he ever commanded another expeditionary force on the Indian frontier.

Churchill cut short his six-week Christmas holiday to sail for India and join Blood on the frontier. Before leaving, he again gained newspaper credentials with the *Daily Telegraph.* This was his opportunity for glory. He wrote, "I have faith in my star—and I intend to do something about it." Now his goal was to write a book and make enough money from it that he could afford to leave the army and stand for Parliament.

In the mountains of Afghanistan, Winston found his battle and his book. Surrounded by hundreds of

Pathan tribesmen, in a scene "like a wild west movie," he later said, Churchill blithely shot his way out with his pistol. In his book, *The Story of the Malakand Field Force,* he wrote: "I found that there is nothing more exhilarating than to be shot at without result." (Almost a century later, President Ronald Reagan quoted those words to his doctors after he had been shot.)

The book came out in 1899 and became a popular read in London political circles. After the Prince of Wales read it, he wrote the author: "My dear Winston, I cannot resist writing a few lines to congratulate you on the success of your book . . . Everybody is reading it, and I only hear it spoken of with praise."

Afghanistan whetted his appetite for more adventure, and he found it in the Sudan, which was then controlled by Egypt. There the Dervishes, a fanatical Islamic sect of suicide warriors, had found a national leader in the Mohammed Ahmed, who called himself the Mahdi (leader of the faithful) and was a turn-of-the-century version of Osama bin Laden. The Dervishes, who had taken Khartoum and executed British General Charles Gordon, threatened southern Egypt. General Horatio Kitchener was dispatched from London to put down the uprising. Again through his mother, Winston gained a position on Kitchener's staff and soon found himself fighting in the last British cavalry charge, at Omdurman. His wartime experience in beating the Dervishes led to another book, *The River War.*

With the £10,000 he had banked from writing, Churchill could finally enter politics. In 1899 he stood for Parliament as the Conservative Party candidate and was adopted by Oldham in a by-election. (In Britain, Parliamentary candidates do not have to be residents of the town they represent; they are often career politicians who have been recommended by the national party.) Oldham, an industrial town near Manchester, was Liberal Party territory, but the Conservatives were trying to make inroads. The son of Lord Randolph and soldier veteran of the famous Sudan cavalry charge gave the party hope. There were two seats in this four-man race. Returning hero Churchill got more attention than the other candidates, but he misunderstood his audience. He dwelled on the continuing glory of the British Empire and ignored the domestic concerns of Lancashire textile workers. In a narrow defeat, he ran third.

Undaunted, Churchill signed on as a war correspondent with the London *Morning Post* to cover the Boer War, which had just broken out in South Africa. The Boers, descendants of the early Dutch settlers (boer means "farmer"), were fighting British colonial rule.

Colonial Turmoil
General Kitchener reviews troops in Khartoum after the defeat of the Dervishes in 1898. Sudan did not gain independence from Egypt until 1954.

CLOSE ESCAPES

Churchill once wrote, "One can see how lucky I was. Over me beat invisible wings." Given his many close calls with death or capture, it's amazing those wings never tired.

In 1895, when he was a military observer in Cuba, rebel gunfire passed inches from his head and cut down the horse immediately behind him.

Two years later, in the high mountains of what is now Afghanistan, 100 Pathan tribesmen ambushed and surrounded him, but he held them off alone.

In the Sudan, he rode into the horses of four-deep sword-wielding fanatics. Officers on either side were hacked to death. Churchill survived.

His escape from prison in the Boer War was lucky indeed. Tired, hungry, and lost, he knocked on a door and announced he was a Dutch clergyman. The burly

Churchill (far right, at the Boer Army prison in Pretoria in 1899) escaped the prison by leaping over a wall while a guard was lighting his pipe. Earlier, his bravery in the Boer War was commended by those who had witnessed him helping to get a derailed British troop train back on the tracks while under heavy fire. In fact, it was during the efforts to save the train that he misplaced his pistol, which left him defenseless and led to his capture.

man at the door said, "If you're a Dutch pastor, I'm the German kaiser. You're Winston Churchill, and there's a price on your head 'Dead or Alive,' and lucky for you this is the only English house within thirty miles."

In World War I, Churchill was supervising trench defenses when he received a note requesting his presence in front of the commanding general. Grumpily he left. A minute later, a bomb obliterated the spot where he had been standing.

When he arrived at Capetown, Churchill immediately looked for a train to the front; he was determined to be the first journalist to cover the fighting. Only an armored troop train was available, but it was reserved for soldiers.

Churchill, however, sneaked on. Along the way, the train was ambushed by the Boer guerrillas. Churchill shed his civilian status and volunteered to organize moving one of the destroyed cars off the track. But the Boers captured him and sent him to prison in Pretoria. He spent his 25th birthday in jail, but twelve days later he escaped over the latrine wall and hopped a freight train. A day later, he found refuge in an English house. A coal-mine manager hid him in a shaft for a couple of days and then packed him in a wool bale on a train en route to Portuguese East Africa.

Churchill then returned to action in time for the British march into Pretoria, where he personally took down the flag of the prison and hoisted the Union Jack.

Two more books flowed from his pen—one about the war and another about his escape. He returned to London in 1900 to find himself a minor celebrity. A London music-hall-performer even sang this ditty:

You've heard of Winston Churchill
This is all I need to say
He's the latest and the greatest
Correspondent of the day

The Conservative Party was anxious to push his candidacy in Oldham once more. When Churchill arrived, the party had bands assembled, playing the tune "See the Conquering Hero Comes." Through streets of cheering thousands, Churchill rode in an open carriage to the town hall. He related the story of his escape from the Boers and laid the credit to a Mr. Dewsnap, the African coal manager's deputy, a native of Oldham whose wife was in the audience. When Mrs. Dewsnap was asked to stand up by Churchill, the audience gave them both an extended roaring ovation. Afterwards, a group of young women presented him with flowers. They wore sashes that said "God Bless Churchill, England's Noblest Hero."

This time around, Churchill knew better than to ignore local issues. He canceled summer vacation with his mother in Scotland and spent the time campaigning in Oldham. Although the town was known as Liberal Party ground, Churchill hit the opposition hard. "The Liberals," he argued, "have no policy of their own, and they do not object to our policy, except they would like to carry it out themselves." On October 1, 1900, Winston Churchill became a Conservative member of Parliament, beating his opponent by just 221 votes.

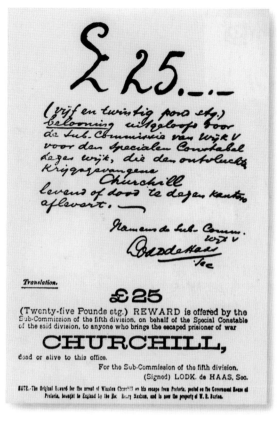

Dead or Alive!

This 1899 wanted poster (written in Afrikaans and English) offers £25 for Churchill "dead or alive." His dramatic escape from South Africa garnered headlines in London and made Churchill a war hero.

Reformer
1900–1910

Churchill took his seat in Parliament in 1900, a year when the voices of Gladstone, Disraeli, and even that of his father, Lord Randolph, still echoed. He tried to pick up his father's standard of "progressive conservatism" or "Tory Democracy." On his third day in the House of Commons, Churchill rose to deliver his maiden speech. The older members frowned as he rose. His father had waited three months before he delivered his first address.

Churchill, who had no particular expertise in any legislature, chose a topic from his own experience: the ongoing Boer War, which Britain would win in 1902. As a veteran of the campaign against the Boer Army, he could get away with expressing sympathy for the Boer cause: "If I was a Boer, I hope I should be fighting in the field for independence." On the Conservative front benches, eyebrows were raised; but then Churchill added:

"If the Boers remain deaf to the voice of reason and blind to the hand of friendship, if they refuse all overtures and disdain all terms, we can only hope that we show determination as strong and endurance as lasting."

One last word remained:

"I cannot sit down without saying how grateful I am for the kindness and patience which the House has heard me and which has extended to me. I well know, not on my own account, but because of a certain splendid memory which many honourable members still preserve."

Churchill had unfurled the standard of Lord Randolph. A year later he again echoed his father by attacking the Conservative government's military budget. "I am very glad, after an interval of fifteen years, to lift the tattered flag I found lying on the stricken field."

Churchill believed that matching Kaiser Wilhelm's budget, pound for pound, in expanding the army was misdirected. Though once a soldier himself, he wanted to beef up the Royal Navy. "Let us turn our individual effort to the Fleet. Why should we sacrifice a game in which we are sure to win to play a game we are bound to lose?" Prime Minister Arthur Balfour was not happy. Balfour left in mid-speech, making a schoolboy face at him as he ducked out.

At 26, Churchill reminded listeners of his maverick father. On his finger, he wore the Marlborough signet ring of his father. During debates, he fingered his gold watch on a chain, the way his father once had. He wore the same polka-dot bow ties as could be found among his late father's possessions at Cumberland House that gave color to the frock suit and wing collar that once were his father's attire. The son had the same stoop, the same gait, the same lurching movement in his walk as his father.

Winston even endeavored to grow a moustache. Lord Randolph's trademark was a big black bushy one, but unfortunately, Churchill's sandy hair was inadequate to the challenge. A contemporary woman who did not approve of his independence from the party line said: "I neither like your new politics or new moustache."

"Madam," replied Churchill, "it is hardly likely you will ever come in contact with either."

Labor Strife

Welsh coal miners (riding a tram during a strike) provided the fuel to run the Industrial Age, but their dangerous work conditions and low pay spurred calls for reform. The left wing of the Liberal Party, led by Welshman David Lloyd George, championed the growing workers' movement.

Indeed, Churchill was now in bad graces with his party. His own constituent association at Oldham had reprimanded him, and he was considering crossing the aisle to sit with the Liberals. The voices of two charismatic orators—one American and one British—were compelling him to switch parties.

In 1903, Bourke Cockran was invited to speak at the Reform Club in London, a bastion of the Liberal Party. Cockran was no partisan of the British Empire or the imperial preferences in trade that it enacted. He was a champion of free trade, which had always been a tenet of the Liberal Party philosophy. Churchill heard Cockran and the two—mentor and pupil—resumed their friendship. By the time he left, Churchill was a free-trader, too.

The second influence was David Lloyd George, the bright new star of the Liberal Party. A fatherless child raised in a Welsh mining town, Lloyd George was becoming the voice of the needy—not only for the coal-mining families in Wales but for workers all over Britain. He had proposals in mind to ease their hardships, and he had the eloquence to make people listen. Winston, the grandson of a duke, found himself swayed.

It was an unlikely partnership. Hardly anyone else in Lloyd George's political circle came from the upper class, who viewed the Welshman as a threat to the social order. But Churchill wryly defended the radical firebrand to his own friends. "David is not against the social order—only those elements of the social order that get in his way."

On May 31, 1904, Churchill crossed the floor of the House of Commons to the Liberal benches. His lucky star must have guided him: the very next year, the Liberals swept out the Conservative government in a landslide. Churchill the convert was rewarded by the new prime minister, Henry Campbell-Bannerman, to a sub-cabinet post—under secretary of state for the colonies.

His former Oldham Conservative association disowned him. So Churchill stood for a seat in Manchester, another working-class city in Central England. There his Conservative opponent, William Joynson-Hicks, was a pious pillar of the Church of England and a supporter of temperance. Joynson-Hicks spoke for the Anglican Church and against whisky, while Churchill was very

DAVID LLOYD GEORGE

Like FDR, Lloyd George took office as a social reformer but gained fame as a wartime leader—in his case, World War I.

The bantamweight David Lloyd George had a mop of white hair and a tenor voice that played on all the strings of the human heart. "He could talk a bird out of a tree," said Churchill of his political mentor. Lloyd George was an unlikely world figure. Born in Wales in 1863 and orphaned a year later, he was raised by his uncle, a shoemaker, in a crude stone cottage. He grew to despise the class system that marked British life, and he championed minimum wage laws, unemployment compensation, health insurance, and a host of other welfare measures that FDR copied more than two decades later.

On the stump, Lloyd George was a fiery speaker who handled hecklers with ease. Once he was speaking on Home Rule. "Home Rule in Ireland, Home Rule in India, Home Rule in South Africa…" he exclaimed, before someone interrupted, "Home Rule for Hell!" "Yes," he said, looking at the heckler, "Home Rule for Hell. I like every man to speak for his own country."

When Lloyd George died in 1945, Churchill called him "the greatest Welshman whom that unconquerable race has ever produced since the age of the Tudors."

much in favor of whisky and ambivalent toward the Church. When Winston campaigned on the Sabbath, his opponent was outraged. But the large Jewish community in Manchester was not. To that audience, he spoke on one Sunday and predicted the creation of the state of Israel. The Jewish vote helped decide his victory.

In 1908, Campbell-Bannerman's death brought in a new prime minister, Henry Asquith, who named David Lloyd George to succeed him as chancellor of the Exchequer. Churchill then assumed Lloyd George's former post as president of the Board of Trade. A new cabinet position, according to British law, requires a new election for the minister. But politics in Manchester had changed by then. For one thing, the Jewish vote had turned against Liberals because they had passed the Aliens Act, which made it harder for Jews on the Continent to immigrate. Meanwhile, Catholic voters were distressed over Churchill's lack of support for Home Rule in Ireland.

Making matters worse were the suffragettes. Although Churchill was not opposed to the concept of women's voting rights, his old-fashioned demeanor did little to reassure women. After being heckled by suffragettes at one appearance, Churchill responded: "I'm not going to be henpecked on a question of such importance." On April 24, he lost the election by 429 votes.

But there was a silver lining to the cloud. One month later, Churchill could hardly believe his good fortune when the Liberal Party assigned him the open seat in Dundee, Scotland, the home of Clementine Hozier. Though they had met briefly four years earlier, the sparks didn't fly until a dinner party in London that March. Winston was in love by the time dessert was served.

Wedding Day
The bride-to-be Clementine Hozier steps out of her carriage at St. Margaret's Church in Westminster in 1908. Churchill's old Harrow headmaster spoke at the service, and King Edward gave Winston a gold cane.

In her porcelain beauty, Clementine reminded Churchill of Ethel Barrymore, the actress with whom he had been briefly smitten. (Barrymore had broken it off before it got serious, saying, "There is only room for one on center stage.") But unlike the stage star, Clementine did not find politics a barrier to romance.

If he could win the seat in Dundee, Winston would be not only romancing the voters of that Scottish seaside city, but wooing his first real love. When Clementine heard the news, she got her grandmother, the Countess of Airlie, to offer her house as the Liberal Party campaign headquarters. The countess used her considerable influence to mobilize her Scottish friends behind Churchill—and the most enthusiastic campaign volunteer was Clementine. She was no stranger to the Liberal Party.

LADY CHURCHILL

Clementine Hozier was born in Dundee, Scotland, in 1885. Although she was the granddaughter of the Earl of Airlie, she grew up in straitened circumstances because her father had divorced her mother when she was six. Partly as a result, she came to prefer the company of politicians and intellectuals, rather than socializing with shallow nobles who led lives of empty pleasure.

She did not like all of Churchill's acquaintances, however, and she minced no words when she felt someone was using him—including the politician Brendan Bracken and Aristotle Onassis. She issued her views on these interlopers in missives written to her husband. But like many couples, their biggest arguments were about money: He was the spender, she was the saver and bill payer. As the loyal and loving wife to a demanding and self-centered

Winston and Clementine (photographed in 1908 for their engagement) lived "happily ever after," in Churchill's own words. She affectionately called him "pig" (he obliged by signing letters to her with a sketch of a pig) and he called her "pushy cat." At age 88, after breaking his hip in Monte Carlo, he wrote to Clementine: "I am a pretty dull and paltry scribbler; but my stick as it writes carries my heart along with it." Once asked in an interview whom he would wish to be other than himself, Winston replied, "Lady Churchill's second husband."

husband, she bore her lot, though not always cheerfully.

Clementine survived Winston by 12 years, living at 28 Hyde Park Gate in London. There she devoted herself to work that burnished her husband's memory, particularly the Churchill Foundation. Most of her income in retirement came from Winston's paintings, which according to his instructions she sold off.

A progressive in politics, Clementine had been a partisan of David Lloyd George before she ever met Winston.

Churchill won the seat, and a month later won her hand, during a weekend trip to Blenheim Palace. Winston knew the palace grounds would be a romantic background for a proposal. Years later when he was asked to recall his greatest speech, Churchill replied: "My greatest address was to an audience of one during a rainstorm in a gazebo at Blenheim. I knew it was the greatest because she accepted." They were married at St. Margaret's Church in Westminster, London, on September 12, 1908.

"I am a child of the House of Commons"

WINSTON CHURCHILL

In short time, the new Mrs. Churchill found that her husband had become in rich circles what she later called "the most hated man" in Britain. With Lloyd George's backing from the Exchequer, Churchill, as president of the Board of Trade, pushed through revolutionary welfare legislation. He pioneered the Labour Exchange as an insurance against unemployment. He enacted an Old Age Pensions Bill and introduced a Miner's Bill that limited work to eight hours. He also got passed a minimum wage bill. He fought for a Scottish small-landholder's bill that let many tenant crofters own their own fields. As he wrote to Lloyd George: "I am fighting a war against poverty."

Poverty may have been Churchill's stated enemy, but his most tenacious foes were the coal barons and the huge estate owners. They felt personally threatened by the new social programs, and they directed their anger not at Lloyd George but at Churchill, who came from their own class. Much like the patrician President Franklin Roosevelt a quarter of a century later, Churchill was labeled a traitor to his class.

As proof of his apostasy, Churchill backed Lloyd George's "People's Budget," which was vetoed by the House of Lords in 1909; and he later campaigned with Lloyd George on his "Peers vs. People" campaign to strip power from the House of Lords.

Prime Minister Asquith found his government embattled. He did not dare to downgrade Lloyd George to another ministry. The Welshman was the idol of the working class, but Churchill was another matter. He had their esteem, but not their affection. It was easier to switch Churchill to another cabinet post, so Churchill was made home secretary in 1910.

In that post, the wrongdoers would be common criminals, not the rich and powerful.

WHISKY, CHAMPAGNE AND CIGARS

"I have taken more out of alcohol than it has taken out of me," said Churchill.

Churchill gained his taste for Scotch whisky as a young officer in South Africa. "The water was not fit to drink," he recalled. "To make it palatable, we had to have whisky. By diligent effort, I learned to like it." In his younger days, he liked Johnnie Walker Black, but he later switched to Dewar's. With champagne, Pol Roger was his choice. When the war ended, Madame Pol Roger communicated to Churchill that her private stock had been hidden from the Nazis and was ready to be shipped to him. That winery even named a bottle in his honor.

In Cuba, Churchill gained his love for the Havana cigar. He smoked about twenty a day, his favorite being Romeo y Julieta by H. Upmann. Yet as Dwight Eisenhower reported: "He never smoked them to the end. Halfway through, he'd light up another."

Yet controversy followed Churchill to the Home Office as well. The country had been paralyzed by a series of strikes, led by the coal miners in South Wales. Churchill, as home secretary, called out troops to help the police quell riots. Four miners were killed. The Welsh workers, who once respected Churchill as Lloyd George's friend, now reviled him as a reactionary. They were not appeased by his past endeavors on their behalf at the Board of Trade.

Churchill's image in some quarters as an agent of repression was not helped by his actions in the so-called "Siege of Sidney Street." Armed radicals led by a Russian anarchist in the poor East End of London attacked a team of "bobbies" from the Metropolitan Police. Home Secretary Churchill was criticized by opponents for appearing at the crime scene and grand standing for a photographer, in what was mostly a matter for the police to handle.

But the tabloid photograph of a top-hatted Churchill astride a fire engine belied the true picture. Churchill had not forgotten the disadvantaged. In the Home Office, he had devoted most of his energies to young offenders whose poverty led them afoul of the law. He championed better conditions of detention and fought draconian sentencing procedures.

For such a young politician, Churchill had already etched an indelible impression on the public. But he had also left in his wake a long line of enemies, from radicals on the left to conservatives on the right. Those among the Tories, the party he had left, were most angered by his joining with Lloyd George on the Welshman's fight to emasculate the House of Lords. As a Liberal, Winston was appalled by the power of veto held by the Lords, who were not elected by the people. On the other hand, dismantling such an august institution also disturbed his sense of tradition. But Churchill swallowed his misgivings and made a speech calling for a radical reform of the House of Lords:

"We see the House of Lords flushed with the wealth of the modern age, armed with a party caucus, fortified, revived, resuscitated, asserting its claims in the harshest and crudest manner, claiming to veto or destroy even without discussion any legislation sent to them by any majority, however large, from the House of Commons."

In response to the attacks, the House of Lords yielded. In the face of a possible packing of the chamber with the creation of new peers, they gave up their veto power. The reform of the House of Lords, the high point of radical Liberal legislation, owed much of its success to Churchill, the grandson of a duke.

The battle over the Lords marked the end of Churchill's radical leanings. Now that the last bastion of aristocratic oligarchy had fallen, Churchill sensed a shift in the mood of the country. If social injustice at home had dominated the political debate, now it was the threat of military aggression abroad. The German kaiser was building up weaponry, expanding his country's influence overseas and putting Britain's nerves on edge. In the competition for the budget, the forces of reform were losing to the armed forces.

The Agadir Crisis of July 1911 gave even more ammunition to the hawks. The German gunboat *Panther* had docked at the Moroccan port of Agadir, and the move was interpreted as an attempt by the Germans to stake out a sphere of influence in North Africa. France and England protested, and the warship became the center of a game of chicken similar to the Cuban Missile Crisis that rattled the world in 1962. During the crisis, while vacationing in Somerset, Churchill found himself haunted by the verse in A. E. Housman's *A Shropshire Lad*. To his wife, he recited from memory:

> On the idle hill of summer,
>   Sleepy with the sound of streams,
> Far I hear the steady drummer
>   Drumming like a noise in dreams.
>
> Far and near and low and louder
>   On the roads of earth go by,
> Dear to friends and food for powder,
>   Soldiers marching, all to die.

Colonial Controversy, European War
Three years after Germany, Britain and France nearly went to war over the Agadir Crisis in Morocco, Moroccan troops like these were defending France in the First Battle of the Marne. On September 9, 1914, the German advance on Paris was halted at the Marne River.

But the soldiers did not march in 1911. Germany receded from the brink. Churchill, though, had glimpsed Armageddon. With his characteristic energy, he began to brief himself on the country's state of military and naval preparedness.

Shortly thereafter, Churchill reached beyond his purview as home secretary and submitted to the Committee of Imperial Defence an astonishingly prescient memorandum titled "Military Aspects of the Constitutional Problem":

"It is assumed that an alliance exists between Great Britain, France, and Russia, and that if these powers are attacked by Germany and Austria, the decisive military operations will be those between France and Germany. . . . The full strength of the Germans . . . will be backed by sufficient preponderance of force, and developed on a sufficiently wide front to compel the French armies to retreat from their positions behind the Belgian frontier . . . The balance of probability is that by the twentieth day the French armies will have been driven from the line of the Meuse and will be falling back on Paris and the south."

Although the army staff called the document "ridiculous and fantastic," in three years it would all happen just as Churchill had predicted. He gave the twentieth day of the German offensive as the day on which the French armies would be driven from the Meuse River, and then forecast that the German army would be fully extended by the fortieth day on all fronts. That is almost exactly what occurred. The First Battle of the Marne was lost by Germany on the forty-first day.

What gave the young Home Office secretary the vision that older and more experienced leaders in the War Office and the Admiralty lacked? Churchill gave a clue when he later described the document in *The World Crisis* as "an attempt to pierce the future; to conjure up in the mind a vast imaginary situation; to balance the incalculable; to weigh the imponderable." The key to Churchill's gift of prophecy was his uninhibited imagination. He was not afraid of making mistakes. Like Christopher Columbus, he could array the facts, sift the possibilities, and with a full calculation of the odds, ride his conclusion far into the horizons of the future. Where the military and bureaucratic mind, confronted by an image of contingencies, would opt for the immediate and safer present, Churchill would weigh each imponderable, gauge the outcome, and proceed to the next step. Casting aside the less probable "ifs," he invaded the veiled future until the course had been resolved. Such a conclusion, unencumbered by qualifications or conditions, became, under the force of Churchill's words and the power of his description, not just a prediction, but a revelation.

The other cabinet ministers were predictably infuriated by Winston's frequent "meddling" in matters considered to be their own jurisdiction.

Lord Haldane

As war secretary, Viscount Haldane (shown in 1914) did not appreciate Home Secretary Churchill's meddling in defense matters. Yet the two men were kindred intellectual spirits: Haldane was also a historian and philosopher.

But Asquith, who as prime minister had the overall responsibility, was increasingly impressed by his thirty-seven-year-old home secretary, the second youngest in history. Not long after his paper on French defenses, Churchill was invited, along with Lord Haldane, the current head of the War Office, to the Scottish summer home of the prime minister.

At the end of the September weekend, Churchill hauled Asquith's daughter Violet from her afternoon tea. "Will you come out for a walk with me at once?" Winston asked her breathlessly.

"You don't want tea?"

"No, I don't want tea. I don't want tea—I don't want anything—anything in the world. Your father has just offered me the Admiralty."

Churchill was overjoyed with the appointment. Destiny, he thought, had been saving him for just such a mission. That night, while undressing for bed, he picked up the Bible on the night table and opened it at random. His eyes lit on this passage:

"Hear, O Israel, Thou art to pass over Jordan this day, to go in to possess nations greater and mightier than thyself, cities great and fenced up to heaven . . . and He shall bring them down before thy face; so shalt thou drive them out, and destroy them quickly, as the Lord has said unto thee."

To Churchill's strongly prophetic mind, it seemed an omen of reassurance.

Navy Days

While he was first lord of the Admiralty, Churchill (entering the House of Commons in 1914) traveled first-class. His office was a luxurious steam yacht, *The Enchantress*, which carried him to every dockyard and naval installation in the British Isles and the Mediterranean.

War Minister
1911–1921

Like a captain given command of his first ship, Churchill joyously threw himself into the task of making the Empire seaworthy against any new challenge or attack. In Britain, the navy is the senior service—it outranks the army, and the first lord of the Admiralty is answerable only to the prime minister. Churchill was going to do more than just clean house; he was going to build a new one. Overboard went old notions of naval practice and precedent. Seniority, which Churchill almost equated with senility, was shoved aside. For the first sea lord (the senior naval commander), he chose Prince Louis of Battenberg, whose special claim to prominence was that he had married Queen Victoria's granddaughter. His German name and accent, however, did not go down well with senior naval officials; neither did the unkept secret of his affair with the notorious beauty Lillie Langtry.

Equally upsetting was his appointment of David Beatty as naval secretary. The young, dashing rear admiral had rankled the stuffy world of the Royal Navy by taking as a bride the brash and beautiful heiress to the Marshall Field department store in Chicago.

Superannuated admirals were not the only ones to be scrapped. Churchill replaced the 13-inch battleship guns with longer range 15-inchers, which had much more devastating power. For speed, he pushed through the development of fast cruisers to supplement the slower, heavily armored Dreadnought-type battleships. And he converted the fleet from coal to oil, which added not only speed but also maneuverability, since it

HORSES

Churchill rides in a hunt in Allogny Forest, near Bourges, France.

"No hour of life is lost that is spent in the saddle," Churchill once wrote, and the statesman himself spent countless hours on horseback. He rode as a soldier in battle, as a polo player in sports, and as a hunter in a fox chase. As a subaltern with the 21st Lancers, Churchill rode in history's last cavalry ride by the British Army, in September 1898. In 1926, as a ranking polo player, he participated in a match in Malta representing England (he was 52 at the time), drawing praise for his horsemanship from competitor Aly Khan. At Chartwell, Churchill kept a stable of horses, including a black stallion racehorse named Colonist II. (His father once raced Colonist I.)

allowed ships to be refueled at sea. He even formed the first fledgling air force in the world, to provide aerial reconnaissance for the fleet.

Churchill had to convince crusty admirals and his fellow cabinet members in the Liberal Party. His reforms cost money—appropriations that would subtract from the budgeted welfare projects David Lloyd George was championing. Lloyd George complained to him: "Winston, you've become a water creature. You think we all live in the sea. All your thoughts are devoted to sea life—fishes and other aquatic creatures. You forget that most of us live on land."

To answer his critics on the left, Churchill said in a speech in Glasgow, the capital of the nation's shipbuilding industry:

"The purpose of British naval power is defensive. We have no thoughts of aggression...There is this difference between British naval power and that of Germany. The British Navy is, to us, a necessity—it is...for them a luxury. Our naval power...is existence to us; it is expansion to them."

If the pacifists in Britain were temporarily silenced, the militants in Germany screamed. The kaiser, voicing their opinions, said: "Why should a big fleet be a luxury to us and a necessity to them?" Churchill's answer to the kaiser was another speech. He proposed "a naval holiday"—a year of no shipbuilding for both nations: "Let us put a blank page into the book of mutual understanding."

There was no reply from Germany. In Britain, public support for Churchill mounted. The cabinet swung behind him. In June 1914, through Churchill's urging, the government bought the majority stock in the Anglo-Persian Oil Company. Then Churchill called a halt to the usual routine maneuvers of the Royal Navy. Instead, he announced "a practice mobilization." Again the intuition of Churchill was incredible. The fleet assembled for action at Spithead, the Royal Navy base.

On June 28 in Sarajevo, Archduke Ferdinand, heir to the throne of the Austrian-Hungarian empire, was assassinated by a Serbian nationalist, setting into motion the events leading up to World War I. In response to the murder, the Austrian army moved its troops into Serbia. Then Russia—long sympathetic

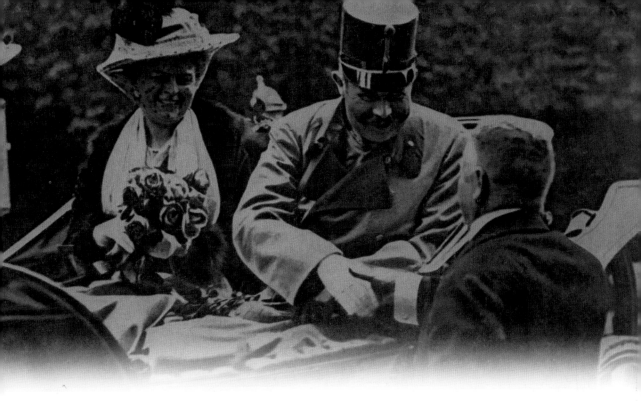

to Balkan nationalists in the Austro-Hungarian empire—declared war against Austria.

Germany was aligned with Austria. That caused Britain, which was worried by a militaristic kaiser, to sign mutual defense treaties with France and Italy—the Triple Entente. Within two months, all of Europe was at war. Britain's specific reason for entering the fray was Germany's invasion of neutral Belgium. The action was popular: A defeat of imperial Germany would take the starch out of the preening kaiser's strut. Just about everyone but Churchill believed the war would be over in weeks.

When war was declared, the British Royal Navy was already on action alert. Churchill dispatched his naval planes, which destroyed some German zeppelin airship sheds and damaged a North Sea submarine base. The raid impressed Lord Kitchener, secretary for war, who asked Churchill to undertake another maneuver. The army wanted to divert the German troops from moving on Dunkirk, the important French harbor on the North Sea, and Churchill was asked to stage a diversionary operation in the Belgian port of Antwerp.

Unlike the army that seeks to do much by stealth, Churchill was asked to do little and parade much. His military excursion would be derided by the press as "The Antwerp Circus."

Asking Churchill to draw attention to himself was like ordering a little boy to put on his first cowboy costume. The uniform he actually arrived in was that of the Elder Brother of Trinity House, an honorific position he held. Its ceremonial costume made him look more like Bonaparte than Buffalo Bill, with its crested plumed helmet and gold-braided uniform. For his trip to Belgium, Churchill commandeered some red London buses and arrived in

Flashpoint of War
The assassination of Archduke Francis Ferdinand (heir to the Austrian throne) and his wife Sophie von Hohenberg reflected Balkan ethnic and political tensions that still trouble Europe.

Antwerp on top of one. In Antwerp, the Belgians cheered as Churchill parked his bus and entered the lobby of his hotel headquarters to assume command.

Finding no Belgian defenses, Churchill took the army, navy, and civil defenses into his own hands. For three days, he was virtually the Belgian chief of staff. He organized darting forays behind German lines. Although Antwerp finally fell, the Circus fulfilled its mission by buying time. As the Belgian King Albert later said: "Because of Churchill, the Germans never took Dunkirk." The French seaport was saved for British ships. Yet Churchill's enemies in England saw the Circus as theatrics. To them, it was Churchill's flamboyance at its worst.

The next time the army called on Churchill for a mission, there were no elements of comedy—only an unrelieved tragedy that is now labeled "the Dardanelles disaster." The Dardanelles are the narrow straits that form the gateway to Istanbul (then Constantinople). Ever since the war began, Churchill had argued for a combined land-and-sea invasion of the Ottoman Empire (now Turkey) to knock the so-called "sick man of Europe" out of the war and shorten the conflict by enabling Russia to attack Germany on its eastern front.

Lord Kitchener was the British secretary for war, whose handlebar moustache adorned England's "Your Country Needs You" posters. (The image inspired James M. Flagg's Uncle Sam poster for the U.S. Army.) It was Kitchener who had suggested the Circus at Antwerp. Now, on New Year's Day 1915, he asked Churchill to seize control of the Dardanelles, which were heavily defended along the Gallipoli Peninsula. Churchill agreed—if it could be a joint military and naval action. But Kitchener didn't keep his side of the bargain, deciding he couldn't spare any of troops from the Western Front. Churchill instead launched the attack alone, and naval firepower was not enough to subdue the Turkish forts on Gallipoli.

Only when the Anzacs (Australians and New Zealanders) became available did the land invasion take place. By then, the Turkish defenses had been reinforced with German machine guns mounted on the hills above the beaches. Casualties mounted to a quarter of a million. Dominion soldiers died on the sands of Gallipoli in fruitless attempt to secure the peninsula. (The Allies eventually withdrew in 1916.) The blame for the carnage was heaped on Churchill, and the scandal gave Conservatives a chance to get back at the turncoat from their ranks. Before they would agree to a wartime coalition government of the Liberal David

"YOUR COUNTRY NEEDS YOU"

Stern Soldier
Lord Kitchener (in this 1914 recruiting poster) was, wrote Churchill, "a gentleman but not a gentle man." His atrocities against the Sudanese in 1898 disgusted Churchill, who also disliked Kitchener's intolerance of Irish Catholics.

Standing on Ceremony
Although Churchill sacked many British naval traditions when he became first lord of the Admiralty, he relished his ceremonial duties. Here he prepares to greet the king and queen upon their return from India in 1912.

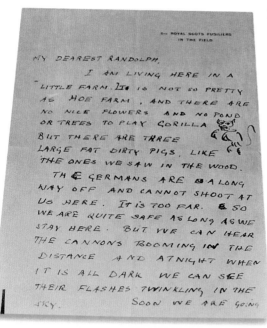

0— ROYAL SCOTS FUSILIERS
IN THE FIELD

MY DEAREST RANDOLPH,

I AM LIVING HERE IN A
LITTLE FARM. IT IS NOT SO PRETTY
AS HOE FARM, AND THERE ARE
NO NICE FLOWERS AND NO POND
OR TREES TO PLAY GORILLA
BUT THERE ARE THREE
LARGE FAT DIRTY PIGS, LIKE
THE ONES WE SAW IN THE WOOD.
THE GERMANS ARE A LONG
WAY OFF AND CANNOT SHOOT AT
US HERE. IT IS TOO FAR. SO
WE ARE QUITE SAFE AS LONG AS WE
STAY HERE. BUT WE CAN HEAR
THE CANNONS BOOMING IN THE
DISTANCE AND AT NIGHT WHEN
IT IS ALL DARK WE CAN SEE
THEIR FLASHES TWINKLING IN THE
SKY. SOON WE ARE GOING

A Letter from the Front
Major Winston Churchill wrote this letter to his 5-year-old son Randolph from the front lines in 1916. The man for whom Winnie the Pooh was named always had a lot of the little boy in him; he loved to embellish letters to his children with whimsical sketches of animals.

Lloyd George as prime minister and Conservative leader Arthur Balfour as foreign secretary, they demanded that Churchill be dismissed from the admiralty. Neither Asquith nor Kitchener was touched by a word of criticism by the Conservatives. By tacit agreement, only Churchill was pilloried as the planner of the disaster. (Yet many authorities believe Constantinople would have been captured without a single casualty if a coordinated Army-Navy attack had been done earlier.)

In disgrace and disgust, Churchill resigned from Parliament and sought a commission in the army at the front. While waiting for his assignment, he went to recuperate in the south of France, still relatively untouched by the war. There the "black dog," the phrase he gave to his bouts of depression, overwhelmed him. Later he told his daughter Sarah that the brutality of his ouster made him feel as if he were "a diver hoisted up from the depths whose veins threatened to burst from the fall in pressure."

Some relief from his pain came in 1916, when he was assigned as major of a battalion on the front lines in Belgium. Although his three months in the trenches saw no major German offensive, he lived almost daily under a barrage of shellfire, which did not seem to rattle him much. He wrote to Clementine about the deadly trench mortars:

"These you can see in the air; & after they fall there is an appreciable interval in which to decide what you will do. I liked these best of all. I found my nerves in excellent order & I do not think my pulse quickened at any time. But after it was over I felt strangely tired: as if I had done a hard day's work at a speech or article."

Now age forty-one, Churchill had developed a notable appreciation for the finer things in life, which presented some problems in the trenches. His portable bathtub and hot-water tank could keep him clean only until the next shell strike covered him in soot. And a good meal was hard to find. A letter to Clementine detailed a care package that was to include "large slabs of corned beef: Stilton cheeses: cream: hams: sardines—dried fruits: you might also try a big beefsteak pie, but not tinned things or grouse."

"Guard them well, admirals
and captains, hardy tars and tall
marines, guard them well
and guard them true."

WINSTON CHURCHILL

AVIATOR

Churchill was an avid pilot, once writing that flying "gives me a feeling of tremendous conquest over space." During World War I, as minister of munitions , Churchill flew daily across the English Channel to keep abreast of needs on the front lines.

Although not a particularly skilled aviator, Churchill was certainly a lucky one. He once survived a crash at a London airfield when his joystick jammed. Another time his plane burst into flames over the Channel, but he managed to glide across to land. He

Flying, like painting, was a form of stress release for Churchill—although his aerial adventures hardly calmed Clementine.

also set a record for the Royal Flying Corps by crashing twice in the same day. That was when Clementine finally put her foot down and ended his aviator days—although as prime minister during World War II, Churchill occasionally took the controls of planes in which he was being flown.

Yet his upper-class tastes did not alienate Churchill from his troops. He tirelessly directed improvements in the foul and bloody trenches, and he worked hard to protect his men. Churchill witnessed firsthand what he called "the disaster of sending armies to chew barbed wire in France and Flanders." He was sickened by the daily attrition of combat that was snuffing out the young men of Britain.

The war had been stalled by the stalemate of trench warfare, and Churchill was not surprised. As a schoolboy, he had predicted such a scenario. But newspaper pictures and accounts of the continuing massacre by machine gun fire when the soldiers went over the top and charged, or by the steady bombardment when they hunkered down in their earthworks, was something else. Churchill's fertile mind went to work. Though his earlier responsibility had been the Royal Navy, he had an idea for the army: an armored land-ship with treads that could make its way across the no-man's land and over the trenches.

HAPPY DAYS

Despite the war raging in Europe, Americans in 1916 enjoyed one of the most prosperous years in history. Factory output soared (in part to supply Europe with goods), wages grew, and farmers prospered. Henry Ford introduced a $250 version of the Model T car, the cheapest ever. Rich folk did well, too: Standard Oil founder John D. Rockefeller became a billionaire that year.

The generals called it "Winston's Folly." They later changed their minds. It would eventually be called the tank because the secret weapon was assembled and built in a storage facility called the tank room.

Shortly after the United States entered the war in April 1917, a parliamentary report cleared Churchill on the Dardanelles disaster. An emboldened Churchill now drafted his critique of the war. He recommended that the government conserve the army's strength until American troops arrived and then move on the German trenches with the tanks he had introduced.

Churchill then sounded out his old constituency at Dundee for a return to the House of Commons. His maneuverings annoyed Prime Minister Lloyd George, who did not relish a tart-tongued Churchill second-guessing the conduct of the war from the back benches. But the prime minister had an idea: Now that America had joined the war, the half-American Churchill might be helpful in expediting arms shipments from the United States. With that argument, Lloyd George sold his cabinet on making Churchill minister of munitions. There, too, Churchill's organizational talents could be harnessed for coordinating the logistics of the soon-to-be-landing Americans.

In his new cabinet role, Churchill was instrumental in deploying tanks at the Battle of Cambrai in November. After just two weeks, the Allies regained 42 square miles of territory held by the Germans, at a cost of just 10,000 Allied casualties—minuscule numbers of dead and wounded compared to the hundreds of thousands lost in other battles. Never again was the offensive force of tanks doubted.

Before the war, Lloyd George had been known abroad as the architect of far-reaching social legislation. But Britain's lead role in the conflict made him even more famous away from home. Photographs of the white-maned prime minister were, for all intents, the face of Britain, and—much like Churchill in World War II—he became the most inspirational figure of the Allied forces. American doughboys returning from France sang a ditty to the tune of "Onward Christian Soldiers": "Lloyd George knows my father; father knows Lloyd George."

Yet at home in Britain, the war effort showed signs of flagging. The slaughter had dragged on

Tank Tactics

Tanks were first used by the British in 1916 at the Battle of the Somme, where they were not deployed decisively and were deemed a failure. But a year later at Cambrai, tanks (including this one) were used in a surprise attack and helped win the battle.

much longer than most Britons had expected, and the casualties kept mounting. Lloyd George knew he could not rally Britain by himself. He needed a surrogate, and he deputized Churchill. In his eighteen months as war minister, Churchill's greatest contribution was his voice. The prime minister's orations were confined to the House of Commons—except for the occasional London banquet. In his place, Churchill crisscrossed England and Scotland, speaking at bond rallies, ship launchings, factories, and civic dinners.

On July 4, 1918, Churchill addressed an Anglo-American dinner and sounded the note that became the closing theme of the war:

"Germany must be beaten; Germany must know she has been beaten. Germany must feel she has been beaten. . . . No compromise with the main purpose, no peace 'til victory, no pact with unrepentant wrong."

The popular press picked up the battle cry: "No peace 'til victory!" The ring of such resolute words squelched the "doubts of 'defeatism,'" a word that Churchill coined to describe the pessimism of war critics.

Victory finally came on November 11, 1918. But Armistice Day found Churchill ambivalent. The carnage had ceased, but he worried about the future. The punitive policies toward Germans disturbed him. "I have always been against the pacifists during the quarrel," he said, "and against the jingoists at its close." To Churchill, the League of Nations was a weak vessel—even more so without the United States, which seemed less than enthusiastic despite the efforts of President Woodrow Wilson. (The U.S. Senate rejected membership in the League of Nations in March 1920.) Lenin's Russian Revolution also troubled Churchill. "Communism is not a policy," he said, "but a disease." He even recommended sending troops to Russia to assist the White Army. The outspoken Churchill was a loose cannon in the cabinet, so Lloyd George decided to channel Churchill's energies in a post that would send him out of London: secretary of state for the colonies.

Specifically, he was charged with negotiating a settlement to bring an end to the conflict in Ireland and the turmoil in the Middle East. "David," Churchill replied, "peace in Ireland and the Holy Land! I am supposed to do in a year what all the prophets, saints,

THREE FOR THE ROAD

Ho Chi Minh as a guerrilla leader around 1940, when Vietnam was under Japanese occupation.

On the August day in 1914 when Britain entered the war against the Central Powers, the first lord of the admiralty asked the chancellor of the exchequer to join him for dinner at the Savoy Hotel. If you count the waiter who took the orders that night, all three men would later be world leaders—and credited with victories in three different wars. The chancellor of the exchequer was David Lloyd George, who became prime minister in 1916 and led Britain to victory in World War I. The first lord of the admiralty was Winston Churchill. And the waiter? He was a Vietnamese student named Ho Chi Minh.

Ho died in 1969—six years before the end of the Vietnam War—but as the founder of his country's Communist Party, he masterminded the revolution that defeated governments backed by France and then the United States.

and diplomats have failed to do for centuries?"

To meet postwar Arab demands in the wake of the defeat of the Ottoman Empire, Churchill called a conference in Cairo with his friend Colonel T. E. Lawrence ("Lawrence of Arabia") as chief advisor. Churchill had once predicted a Jewish homeland in Palestine, and he wanted to fulfill the Balfour Declaration in 1917, which promised just that. He had noted the fleeing Jewish refugees from Communist Russia.

But Churchill was worried about the safety of Jews in Palestine. To check the more anti-Zionist factions of Islam, he maneuvered to put two members of the royal Faisal family, known for its more moderate views, on the Middle East thrones of Iraq and Jordan. In the Cairo Treaty, Jews could return to their Palestine homeland and begin the rebuilding of Zion.

Irish Treaty
When Michael Collins signed the Irish peace treaty in 1921, Ireland was granted dominion status, like Canada and Australia. After Churchill was attacked by old-line Tories for engineering the treaty, he replied: "Ireland is not a daughter state but a parent nation."

Ireland was another postwar hotbed. As first lord of the Admiralty in 1912, Churchill had helped ease Protestant Northern Ireland's defiance over Home Rule. This time, however, the threat of rebellion came from the Catholic south. Dublin was now scorning the offer of Home Rule. Instead, the island's Catholic political leaders wanted total independence—and they were prepared to fight for it. The Irish Republican Army, whose troops were then less like terrorists and more like soldiers, was conducting a full-scale civil war.

Unlike his father, who proudly proclaimed, "Ulster is right and Ulster will fight," Winston sympathized with Irish aspirations. "Why should we expect the Irish to be like the English?" he once asked. "They have their own history, their own language, their own culture." Yet Churchill's strategy for peace was far from peaceful. It included some fair and generous terms, but they were combined with the threat of force and the flash of rhetoric.

As was so often the case, Churchill's straightforward personal style became his greatest asset. When he first met with Michael Collins, the Irish nationalist who had led the Easter 1916 uprising, Collins said, "You hunted me day and night. You put a price on my head."

"Wait a minute," said Churchill, pulling out a framed copy of the reward offered by the Boers for his own head. "At least you got a good price—£5,000. Look at me; £25 dead or alive. How would you like that?"

The relationship between the old soldiers ripened into one of mutual respect. Churchill handed Collins and other leaders the alternative of Dominion status (like that of Canada and Australia) or war. Collins knew the fury that would erupt from his own people by signing. As Collins penned his name, he said, "I expect soon to be killed." He was right. Before his assassination, Collins wrote one last message: "Tell Winston we could never have done it without him."

The gains for peace in Ireland came at a price. The Irish treaty shattered the Conservative Party's support of Lloyd George's coalition. The government fell, and a new election was held. On the day of the general election in 1922, Churchill found himself convalescing in a Dundee hospital from an attack of appendicitis, which had cut short his electioneering. When the returns came in, Churchill, in a hospital bed, was listening to a new contraption called the wireless. He shook his head at the landslide defeat and said to his nurse:

"All of a sudden, I find myself without a party, without a ministry, without a seat—and even without an appendix."

Lawrence of Arabia
T. E. Lawrence (second from left, behind Prince Feisal, later King of Iraq, at the Paris Peace Conference of 1919) was, according to Churchill, "not in complete harmony with the normal." A mystic and a recluse who nonetheless relished publicity, Lawrence mastered what Churchill called "the art of backing into the limelight."

Conservative Chancellor

1922–1930

Although it seems hard to believe given what we know today, the defeated Churchill in 1922 was considered a relic of the past. He was forty-eight years old and no longer a young man of promise. His hair, still sandy, had thinned and made no pretense of covering the scalp; his slouch, which once gave his youth a purposeful cast, now seemed less a mannerism than a mirror of age. The days of adventure and greatness seemed behind him. At that time of life when most men find the security of career replacing the dreams of youth, Churchill had neither. The moorings were missing—not only those of politics and party, but the personal ones of property and household.

For most of his life, Churchill had been rootless. He had fought in many countries, occupied many ministerial posts, and lived in many houses and apartments. Now, as head of a growing family, he yearned to settle down, to seek the solace of the countryside in a home that was his own, where his children could run and romp.

On a November Sunday in 1922, he took his family on a drive from London to see an estate in Kent. Not until their return did he grinningly reveal that the old mansion, Chartwell, was already theirs; he had bought it with the proceeds of a recent inheritance from his great-grandmother, the Marchioness of Londonderry.

The children had loved the house, but Clementine repressed her reaction and was silent on their return ride to London. Then, in the privacy of their bedroom, she erupted. How could Churchill

CHARTWELL

When Churchill acquired Chartwell in 1922, the rambling Tudor mansion and its grounds were in poor condition, which explains the bargain-basement price of £5,000. But the view was splendid—a hilly crown wooded by spreading chestnuts and sturdy oaks overlooking the green of an English meadow. It was a scene he later loved to paint.

Churchill threw himself into the task of restoring Chartwell, starting with the grounds. He cut back overgrown ivy to reveal the Tudor lines, dredged out a pond for swimming and as a focus for his painting, and built brick retaining walls. The house itself suffered from overenthusiastic previous renovations—a hallmark of the anything-goes Victorian era. Much as Churchill the speechwriter would strike out the clumsy word, or revise the awkward sentence, so did Churchill the homeowner hack off ornamental gables and slice away ponderous

Chartwell took its name from a clear spring that provided water to the house. While working on its renovation, Churchill rented a nearby house called Hosey Rigge, which he dubbed "Cosy Pig."

oriel windows. Soon the handsome manor, stripped down to its pre-Victorian lines, was blending seamlessly into the pastoral Kent countryside.

Churchill once wrote: "We shape a dwelling and it shapes us." The remodeled house, with its ample library shelves, became his base for research and preparation in his years of exile from office. The steady stream of guests—some overnight—were visitors from Germany and Europe, military experts on aviation, scientists and engineers working on new weaponry, and politicians whom he could convince on Britain's need to rearm. Today Chartwell is a museum operated by the British National Trust.

put down the money for a new house without consulting her? It was all well and good to say that the children needed a country house, but she saw it more as an excuse for grand-scale weekend entertaining for his friends, which they could little afford—not to mention the fact that she would have to do all the work.

But Clementine quickly forgave her impulsive husband. She had to admit that the new house would be fun for their growing family. Clementine that year gave birth to their last child, Mary. (Today, that daughter, Lady Soames, is the only surviving child of Winston Churchill.) The oldest child, Diana, was now thirteen. Randolph was eleven and Sarah eight. A three-year-old daughter, Marigold, had died the previous year in 1921.

Even though he was out of office, Churchill still had many speech requests to honor, as well as writing contracts to fulfill. Yet he did not neglect his children. Nor did he find it difficult to communicate with them, as his father had with him. Perhaps it was the little boy that never entirely left Winston. The make-believe games and imaginary playmates of the children found a ready listener and participant in their father. Unlike the typical English father, who seemed to dote only on his dog, Churchill was affectionate with his children (and his pets). Visitors to Chartwell noted the impishness and playfulness in Churchill that found a ready response from his children. In 1924 one of his friends, A. A. Milne, gave Churchill's name to his famous creation—Winnie the Pooh. ("Pooh" was how Milne's baby son said "bear.")

Yet Churchill was restless. For the first time since 1900, his voice was absent from the national scene. He yearned to be part of the political action. But in what party should he place his hopes and aspirations? The Liberals? That party was a mere shell of the coalition that had dominated Britain for so many years. It was now shattered into splinters by the pro–and anti–Lloyd George factions. A head without a body, it had become the party of preachers, teachers, and intellectuals. Except for some pockets of strength in Wales and Scotland, the mass of English workers had deserted it for the Labour Party, which was now the party of the future on the left. Its leaders claimed kinship with the "brother socialists" in Russia—blind to the brutalities of Lenin's totalitarian regime. In addition, the Labourite plan for the state ownership of industries repelled Churchill.

Union Man
When a local union objected that Churchill the bricklayer (here seen working at Chartwell) was not a member of the stonemasons' guild, the politician stepped up his pace to three bricks a minute to qualify as a pro. He paid his dues and joined the union.

So did the concept of enforced egalitarianism. "The American Declaration of Independence says: 'all men are created equal,' " said Churchill, "but the socialists say: 'all men should be kept equal.' I'm all for equality at the starting gate but not at the finish line."

By process of elimination, that left the Conservative Party. In his heart and mind, Churchill would always be a "Tory Democrat" in the mode of Lord Randolph and Disraeli. The word "Tory" was an epithet hurled by the left at the Conservatives, but many old-family Brits wore it as a badge of pride. Those who liked to call themselves Tories were the grand ladies in big hats who organized town charity bazaars, or the men in pink riding attire who chased foxes, as well as those who wore red flowers in their lapels on "Poppy Day" to show their support for veterans. They carried deep convictions of noblesse oblige, which allowed them to endorse many social-welfare programs, as did Churchill.

"Implacable Vengeance"

Churchill abhorred Russian Communist leader Vladimir Lenin (in a Soviet propaganda poster), whom he described as having "implacable vengeance rising from frozen pity," and he had no patience for Bolshevik sympathizers in Britain.

On the other hand, the rising class of self-made rich men—the corporate chieftains and merchants, as well as those who worked at Lloyds Insurance or Barclays Bank, were not so fond of the Tory designation. Steeped in laissez-faire economic philosophies, these businessmen were unlikely to support public programs in health and education.

Churchill had some problems with big business, but now he was coming to believe that big trade-union heads were becoming even more autocratic and irresponsible with their demands than the heads of industries. So Churchill asked to be accepted back into the Conservative Party. Alas, the Conservatives did not want him. He had ratted on them in 1904, they said, and now he wanted to "re-rat."

Still Churchill persisted in his overture to the Conservatives. He asked them to adopt him as a candidate when a vacancy arose in the historic seat of Westminster. This key constituency was right in the heart of London and included Westminster Abbey, the Houses of Parliament, 10 Downing Street, and the cabinet ministries at Whitehall. Predictably, he was turned down.

Undaunted, Churchill created his own one-man Constitutionalist Party and took on the political establishment in what may have been the most colorful campaign in British parliamentary history.

It was certainly the oddest collection of volunteers a British election has ever seen. The constituents of the district included the street toughs of Soho, the theater set of the Strand, poor folks and peers—and Churchill mobilized them all. Duchesses in diamonds went door-to-door. Showgirls stayed up all night after performances stuffing envelopes. Jockeys in silks and prizefighters in trunks took to the stump for Churchill. Their rallying cry was "the man against the machine." Churchill himself introduced a posh version of the sound truck to England, except his was a carriage drawn by four horses with a standing trumpeter blaring out the candidate's arrival. One American (although the wife of a Conservative Party member of Parliament) hung huge posters in her London town-house windows that showed a picture of Churchill's newest child, Mary, with the caption: "Vote for my daddy."

If Londoners and the newspapers, nearly all of which endorsed Churchill, warmed to the American-style campaign, Churchill glowed. In his earlier races, he had been constrained by party rules, but this time he could be himself. He had a cause: he would show the hidebound Tories and the shrinking Liberals alike how to fight Socialists. "The British people," he said, "are not going to slide and slither weakly and hopelessly into Socialist confusion."

In another talk, he charged:

"In a few weeks a Bolshevik ambassador will reach these shores and be rapturously welcomed by the Socialist minister. He will be applauded by every revolutionary and will be conducted to the presence of the sovereign. He represents a government which has reduced a mighty and noble nation to a slavery never witnessed since the Middle Ages."

"Mary the Mouse"
Churchill doted on his youngest child, Mary (in a 1928 photo), nicknaming her "Mary the Mouse." When her pug fell ill he wrote a ditty for her that began: "Oh what is the matter with poor puggy wug? Pet him, kiss him, and give him a hug."

> ## "Expenditure always is popular; the only unpopular part about it is the raising of money to finance the expenditure."
>
> WINSTON CHURCHILL

But it was not to be. Despite the spectacular campaign, Winston lost by forty-three votes. Yet wrapped in the defeat was a victory. Churchill had fought his way back to the national spotlight. The Conservative Party leader, Stanley Baldwin, recognized Churchill's potential power. After all, a former Conservative prime minister, the venerable Arthur Balfour, had endorsed

NINE PRESIDENTS

Nixon (meeting Churchill in 1954) called the British leader "the largest human being of our time."

Over a political career that spanned the reigns of Queen Victoria and Queen Elizabeth, Churchill met nine current or future American presidents. The first was Theodore Roosevelt, a distant cousin of his mother, in December 1900. The governor of New York had just been elected vice president as William McKinley's running mate the month before. Churchill was impressed by T. R.'s mind and energy, but the feeling was not reciprocated. "They were too much alike," wrote Roosevelt's daughter Alice. "Father looked upon Winston as the former debutante looks at the prize beauty in the new year's crop."

In Washington shortly thereafter, Churchill warmed to the genial President McKinley, who reminded him of his grandfather, the Duke of Marlborough.

Churchill next met Woodrow Wilson, at the Versailles Conference in 1919. He was no admirer of Wilson, whom he felt was ineffective. "He was all for peace and good will to nations abroad," said Churchill, "but if he had applied that to Republicans at home, he might have got the League of Nations passed."

Churchill visited Herbert Hoover at the White House in 1929, but there was no chemistry between the ebullient Brit and the dour Midwestern mining engineer.

Franklin Roosevelt was obviously his favorite president, although Eisenhower was not far behind. And Churchill admired Truman for his plain-spoken approach—even if the Missourian found Churchill a bit long-winded.

Churchill also met John Kennedy when the Harvard student took a year off to work with his father, Ambassador Joseph Kennedy, in London. (He also spoke to President Kennedy over the telephone.) Finally, Churchill met Vice President Richard Nixon twice in the 1950s and was impressed with his grasp of world affairs.

Churchill's effort as an independent. So the Conservatives offered Churchill a safe seat in the election next year.

When the Conservatives, along with Churchill, swept into office on October 29, 1924, Baldwin—the new prime minister—summoned Churchill to 10 Downing Street. "Well, Winston," asked the bluff Yorkshireman between puffs on his pipe, "will you take the chancellorship?"

Churchill thought he meant the chancellor of the Duchy of Lancaster—a ceremonial sinecure with no power. But so eager was he to be back in the Conservative councils, Churchill said yes. Not until later did he realize it was chancellor of the Exchequer.

The chancellor of the Exchequer lives at 11 Downing Street (next door to the prime minister) and is the number-two man in government. But the position carries far more power and prestige than the vice presidency of the United States. In fact, the chancellor of the Exchequer has the prestige of the chief justice of the Supreme Court—and the powers of the secretary of the Treasury, the budget director, head of the IRS, and the chairman of the Federal Reserve rolled into one.

The Conservative Party's prodigal son had been awarded the government's most coveted appointed seat. For his ceremonial investiture, Churchill donned the same black robes that Lord Randolph had once worn as chancellor. His mother had carefully saved them for her son.

The robes fit, but the chancellorship did not suit Winston, a man who could not even manage his own finances. Being the foreign secretary would have been a better fit. Maps on his desk were one thing, balance sheets another. As a young man Winston described his befuddled approach to the mysterious realm of mathematics:

"We arrived in an *Alice-in-Wonderland* world at the portal of which stood 'A Quadratic Equation' followed by the dim chambers inhabited by Differential Calculus, then a strange corridor of Sines, Cosines, and Tangents in a highly square-rooted condition."

For the first time in his ministerial career, he was wholly dependent on his advisers, the career bureaucrats of the Exchequer department. Virtually every British economist—into whose ranks a dubious heretic named John Maynard Keynes was not admitted—recommended that the cure to Britain's unemployment slump was a draconian diet of reduced spending and a return to the gold standard. This deflationary move was the singular, if questionable, achievement in Churchill's four-year supervision of the depressed economy.

Economics may be "the dismal science," as historian Thomas Carlyle wrote, but Churchill was determined to enliven the field. On the occasion of his first presentation of the budget, Churchill paused and filled his glass beside him. What came out of the carafe was not a crystal stream of water

Indecisive Leader
Churchill was grateful to Prime Minister Stanley Baldwin (shown in 1926) for bringing him back into council. But he often quarreled with Baldwin, who he felt was an indecisive leader.

but something more amber in color. Churchill announced: "It is imperative that I should first fortify the revenue, and this I shall now do." He paused before sipping the whisky. "With the permission of the Commons, I now do." To the cheers of the house, he took a drink.

Considering the times in which he presided, Churchill might be forgiven for resorting to spirits. Labor unrest had led to a general strike in 1926. Everything shut down; the country was at a standstill. Churchill took a hard line against the strike. "I declare utterly not to be impartial between the fire brigade and the fire." When the London newspapers quit publishing, ex-journalist Churchill strode into the void and set up his own newspaper, the *British Gazette*. For eight days, Churchill—in green eyeshades and a pair of sleeve garters—bawled out directions for turning out the daily edition. He was at that time the preeminent news dispenser in England, with a circulation of 1,000,000. His plans for expansion were developing when the strike ended.

Generally, though Churchill's stint at the Exchequer was not a happy one. Financial orthodoxy did not inspire his genius, and the everyday burden of mastering budgetary details began to weary him. He commented later: "They said I was the worst chancellor in history and, you know, they were right."

The country muddled along economically until 1929, when the United States and the world were blanketed, in Churchill's words, by an "economic blizzard." In the wake of market crashes and the onset of the Great Depression, the Conservatives were swept out of office. Churchill himself was reelected, but under the new Labour-led government, he had no ministry or cabinet posts. In British political terms, while still a member of Parliament, he was considered "out of office." He remarked, "I'd quit politics altogether if it weren't for the chance that someday I might be prime minister."

General Strike

During the disastrous eight-day General Strike of 1926, six million British workers walked off their jobs. Not a bus, truck, nor train moved. Steel factories were closed, and ships could not unload.

AN APPETITE FOR LIFE

"My idea of a good dinner is first have good food, then discuss good food," said Churchill.

If few world leaders could match wits with Churchill, even fewer could keep up with him at the table. A Churchill breakfast generally consisted of melon, eggs, and bacon—followed by a veal cutlet, fried bread with marmalade, and plenty of coffee and cream.

Lunch on the same day might start with a fillet of sole wrapped in smoked salmon and garnished with shrimp, then roast venison stuffed with pâté de foie gras and served with a truffle sauce.

Then came dinner, when he really got serious. This is an actual dinner that Sir Winston enjoyed at the Savoy Hotel in his eighty-eighth year: He opened with oysters and champagne, followed by a pea purée and a glass of sherry. Then he attacked a poached turbot in cream sauce, washed down with some Pouilly-Fuissé. The next course was beef Wellington with a side of carrots and scalloped potatoes, along with a bottle of burgundy. Dessert was crème brûlée with a glass of Madeira. And finally, he called for Stilton cheese and a glass of port. After coffee, he concluded the repast with a cigar and brandy. Breakfast, anyone?

Wilderness Prophet
1931–1939

Out of office in 1931, Churchill now moved from his chambers at the Exchequer to his library at Chartwell. There his library shelves groaned under the weight of more than 6,000 books. Biographies were arranged alphabetically, histories by country, novels by author, along with numerous reference books. They became the tools of his trade, as Churchill's interests now turned from current events to writing a biography of his ancestor, Sir John Churchill (1650–1722), the first Duke of Marlborough. It wasn't his only writing project. He lived, in his words, a "pen-to-mouth" existence, and not a bad one—earning about £20,000 ($100,000) annually writing pieces for magazines, including *Colliers* in America. Churchill's writing was much sought after, in part because a decade earlier he had authored *The World Crisis,* the best-selling first volume of his history of World War I. Not everyone found it a good read. In a slap at Churchill's frequent mention of himself, Lord Balfour, the former prime minister and foreign secretary, described it as an "autobiography disguised as a world history."

In *Marlborough,* Churchill told the story of how the duke defeated Louis XIV. The Bourbon monarch—who styled himself "The Sun King"—had endeavored to make Europe his own personal empire. The subject was hardly academic in the 1930s. From Adolf Hitler's early speeches, Churchill sensed that another megalomaniac's ambitions endangered the stability of Europe.

LADY ASTOR

Churchill once told Lady Astor (pictured here in 1946), "When you first entered the House, I felt you had come on to me in my bath and I had nothing to protect me but my sponge."

The first woman to be elected to the House of Commons was an American at that—Lady Nancy Astor (1879–1964). From an old Virginia family, she took her husband's place in Parliament when he advanced to the House of Lords on his father's death. (The elder Astor, descended from the New York family, had moved to Britain, where his philanthropy had been rewarded by a peerage.)

Churchill clashed frequently with Lady Astor, a Christian Scientist with strong views against alcohol. Once, when Churchill spotted Astor entering the chamber while he was speaking, he paused to fill his water glass. "It must be a great pleasure for the noble lady, the member for Sutton, to see me drink water," he said.

Even harder for Churchill to swallow were Astor's pro-German views: Before the war, she regarded Hitler as a responsible nationalist. Once during a dinner at her home, Astor playfully told Churchill: "If you were my husband, I'd put poison in your coffee." Churchill replied, "And if I were your husband, I'd drink it."

Churchill told the House of Commons that the marching of young German men in uniform and the new stockpiles of weaponry were omens that Britain could ill afford to ignore.

In Parliament, Churchill was now a so-called backbencher, meaning that he was not allowed to sit in the front row seats of the House of Commons, where the cabinet resides with the the prime minister, the chancellor of the Exchequer, and the foreign secretary. In short, a backbencher is not a member of the inner circle. He is never consulted on policy matters and is therefore free to attack the positions taken by the government. But there are risks: If he votes too many times with the opposition, his own party constituency may "un-adopt" him as their member, in which case he would have to stand for reelection under another party—assuming one would adopt him.

Stanley Baldwin had become prime minister again in 1935. Churchill did not seek nor receive a cabinet post or ministry in Baldwin's government.

The state of the British Empire now dominated House of Commons debate and the press headlines. The "crown jewel" of the Empire was India. Baldwin and his viceroy in India, Lord Halifax, had worked out a settlement to give India its political freedom, in response to mounting protests and riots led by Nehru and Gandhi, the Hindu ascetic.

> "Every prophet has to go into the wilderness. He must serve a period of isolation and meditation. This is the process by which psychic dynamite is made."
>
> WINSTON CHURCHILL

From the backbenches, Churchill roared his opposition. India, he said, was "not a political but a geographical term." There were "fifty different Indias" and only Britain could hold the balance between them. He predicted that as many as a million people might be killed in religious conflicts between the Hindus and Moslems. In his attack against the government bill, Churchill charged: "Democracy is the argument the government uses, but aristocracy would be the result—an India run by Brahmin-born elites like Nehru and Gandhi, whose caste treatment of the 'untouchables,' the lower classes, is brutal in their harshness."

But there was more to Churchill's opposition than concern for "the untouchables." In Churchill's mind, losing India was the first step in dismantling the Empire. Britain without an Empire, to Churchill, was like Samson shorn of his locks; the Empire was the source of Britain's strength as a world power.

With hindsight, Churchill's prewar opposition to Indian independence can be characterized as reactionary. In fairness, though, he truly believed that a people with no tradition or history of civil liberties would experience corruption and strife if exposed to democracy prematurely. Indeed, his prediction of violent religious conflicts came true after a Labour

The India Question
A political cartoon mocks Churchill's paternalistic view toward India—an attitude that became increasingly out of sync with public opinion.

government finally granted India its freedom in 1947. In time, of course, India proved Churchill wrong; although cultural and religious unrest continues, the country remains the world's largest democracy.

But in 1935, Churchill's fervent opposition won the day. The government's bill to grant India autonomy was defeated, and Churchill's tenuous relations with Baldwin were frayed further. But then something much closer to home made matters worse between them.

In 1936, Churchill backed King Edward VIII in his marriage to a divorced American, Mrs. Wallis Simpson—just as the prime minister was orchestrating the king's abdication. During the nine-day abdication crisis, Churchill was impulsively romantic, staunchly loyal to his longtime friend, the former Prince of Wales. Churchill urged Edward to play for time against a prime minister who insisted that marriage to Simpson would mean the end of the monarchy. At one speech on Edward's behalf, Churchill was heckled: "Sit down, twister. Sit down."

Edward chose to give up the throne, which turned out to be fortunate for the nation; he was much too shallow and sybaritic to head a nation on the verge of war. Churchill went to Edward's retreat at Fort Belvedere and helped him compose the abdication speech. Among the phrases Churchill contributed were "bred in the constitutional tradition by my father" and "one matchless blessing, enjoyed by so many of you and not bestowed on me—a happy home with wife and children." As Churchill bade him farewell, the king noticed there were tears in his eyes. "I can still see him," wrote Edward later, "standing at the door, hat in one hand, stick in the other." Churchill was tapping out the solemn verse from Andrew Marvell (which was written about Charles I's execution):

He nothing common did, or mean,
Upon that memorable scene.

Churchill was an ardent monarchist because he believed that the monarchy was an effective barrier against dictatorship. What Churchill wisely realized was that in the modern constitutional monarchy of Great Britain, power was divorced from pomp and ceremony—unlike what was happening in Germany at the time. It is a principle that continues to this day. British prime ministers do not rate motorcades and military reviews; their workday existence is starkly different from the glamorous life of the monarch, who is head of

Edward and Wallis

The Duke and Duchess of Windsor on their wedding day, June 3, 1937, at the Chateau de Condé in Tours, France. The marriage ended a scandal that had briefly threatened the monarchy.

BRUSH WITH FAME

Landscape painting was Churchill's escape from the pressures of office, and a way to reenergize his thoughts. "The tired parts of the mind," he said, "can be rested and strengthened not merely by rest but by using other parts."

Churchill began to experiment with oils in France after his dismissal from the Admiralty during World War I, at first dabbling with his daughter Sarah's paint set. When the English artist Sir John Lavery found Churchill daintily contemplating a blank canvas, he took the brush and boldly splotched on a mass of paint. "You see," Lavery told Churchill, "it does not strike back." Churchill got the message, and began attacking art with his usual ferocity.

Churchill (painting a landscape in France in 1948) once noted, "When I get to heaven I mean to spend a considerable portion of my first million years in painting and to get to the bottom of the subject."

Over the years he became an accomplished artist. Under the *nom de brush* Charles Moran, Churchill had paintings exhibited in the Louvre. Churchill even convinced Eisenhower to take up painting—advising him, "Ike, I never paint people, only trees and mountains because they don't talk back." Eisenhower ignored the advice on subject matter: He once did a portrait of Churchill.

state, yet not a politician. The British monarch is thus a unifying figure above politics—and for Churchill, the disenthronement of King Edward VIII endangered the institution of the monarchy.

Although his reasoning was sound, Churchill bet on the wrong horse, in this case. Edward could flash a superficial charm, but he had neither the character nor the moral fiber of his younger brother George VI (father of Queen Elizabeth), who replaced him. In fact, in the late 1930s, the ex-king allowed himself to be manipulated by the Nazis. Churchill later admitted his error of judgment in the Edward affair.

Just after the abdication, when Churchill became a pariah in his own party, his friend, the socialist writer George Bernard Shaw offered Churchill two tickets to the opening of his new play, *The Millionairess.* "Bring a friend, Winston," he added, "if you have one."

Churchill looked at his calendar and replied: "Unfortunately, G.B.S., I have another engagement on that night. But I would like to come to the second night—if there is one." Churchill, however, enjoyed the Irish playwright. When Churchill received his Nobel prize for literature in 1953, he noted that two other British authors had been similarly honored: Shaw and Rudyard Kipling. "One liked me but not my politics. The other's politics I liked, but he didn't like me." (Kipling, a Conservative and a cousin of Stanley Baldwin, thought Churchill was too full of himself.)

Churchill did not improve his popularity by continued warnings about Hitler's rising menace. To an economically depressed nation that had just lost half its young men in World War I, calls for rearmament and the warnings of the threat of another world conflict were messages few wanted to hear.

But Churchill believed someone had to hold the facts up to the light. So in 1932, he delivered this warning about the Hitler government: "We watch with surprise and distress the tumultuous insurgence of ferocity and war spirit and the pitiless treatment of minorities."

A year later, Churchill told the House of Commons: "I regret to hear the undersecretary say we were only the fifth air power in the world and that the Air Ministry has not produced a single plane in the past year." He concluded: "The march of events is passing us by."

There was nothing cursory or casual about these speeches. Churchill prepared like a scholar, studying reams of papers and statistics on comparative defenses, which he then cast in the light of history. As a result,

"G.B."

Playwright George Bernard Shaw was a pacifist who traveled to Moscow in 1936 and praised the communism of Stalinist Russia. Despite Shaw's political differences with Churchill, the two men were friends who respected each other's quick wit.

his speeches were invested with an intellectual and emotional force that no politician who relies on speechwriters can achieve. Churchill's words were his very being.

By 1935, Hitler's militaristic march grew louder. He tore up the Versailles Treaty and instituted a draft of Germany's young men. The next year, his troops paraded into the Rhineland, and he proclaimed his Axis alliance with Italy's fascist leader, Benito Mussolini. Baldwin's response to Hitler's saber-rattling was his personal pledge of peace. "I give you my word there will be no great armament in this country."

At Chartwell, Churchill was organizing what a young Conservative member of parliament, Harold Macmillan, called "a government in exile." Macmillan, a future prime minister, described Churchill's study as filled with maps, charts, and graphs denoting productions of German munitions. Filing cabinets bulged with folders detailing German warplanes and profiles of Hitler's top henchmen, such as Goebbels and Himmler, as well as key German generals. One day the French statesman Paul Reynaud would arrive at Chartwell and run into British scientist Frederick Cherwell on his way out. The constant stream of dining guests and overnight visitors exhausted Clementine. She told family and friends: "The epitaph on my gravestone will read: 'Here lies a woman who was always tired/trying to do all the things that were required.'"

If Mrs. Churchill was at times exhausted, her husband was ever energized. Now he had the ammunition for his argument. Time for Britain was running out, and he had the data to prove it. Some of his warnings focused on the German superiority in the air. In 1935, he told the House of Commons: "Germany has the power at any time henceforward to send a fleet of planes capable of discharging in a single voyage at least 500 tons of bombs on London." But the government dismissed the threats and delayed equipping the depleted Royal Air Force. In 1937, Churchill savaged Baldwin for his weak-kneed vacillation:

"The government cannot make up their minds, or they cannot get the prime minister to make up his

BERNARD BARUCH

Bernard Baruch enjoying a quiet moment in London's St. James's Park.

Bernard Baruch was an American stockbroker and advisor to world leaders for much of the 20th century. Although politically a conservative Democrat, Baruch was nonpartisan in his advice, gaining the confidence of presidents from Woodrow Wilson to Dwight Eisenhower. Eleanor Roosevelt called him "the wisest man I know." The press dubbed him the "park-bench philosopher," for his habit of pondering the problems of the world from a bench in Lafayette Park across from the White House.

Baruch and Churchill became friends during World War I, when Churchill was minister of munitions and Baruch served on the American War Industries Board. As such, Baruch had the power to provide Britain with ammunition, and he stayed in constant touch with Churchill. After the stock market crash of 1929, Baruch took over Churchill's investments. Churchill often stayed at his New York apartment on East 66th Street between the wars. The two men were both in their 90s when they died in the same year.

mind. So they go on in strange paradox, decided only to be undecided, resolved to be unresolute, adamant for drift, solid for fluidity, all-powerful to be impotent."

A little later, when Baldwin fell ill, a Conservative member lamented to backbencher Churchill: "What would happen if our beloved Stanley would die?"

Churchill replied: "Embalm, cremate, and bury him—take no chances." Across the political spectrum, reaction to Churchill's call to arms ranged from skittish to spineless. The leader of the Labour Party said Britain should disarm as an example to Hitler, and the leader of the Liberals compared Churchill to a "Malay tribesman running amok." Still, Churchill insisted that British politicians were frittering away their chances to rearm. The 1930s were, in Churchill's phrase, "the lotus years," when Britain wasted all its opportunities to prepare.

Chartwell Study

"If you cannot read all your books, at any rate handle, or as it were, fondle them," said Churchill (pictured at Chartwell in 1939). "Set them back on their shelves with your own hands, so that if you do not know what is in them, at least you know where they are."

During these Chartwell years, his enemies circulated rumors that an over-the-hill Churchill was sliding into habitual drunkenness. Churchill did nothing to quell these stories. Unlike the alcoholic who carefully conceals his number of drinks, Churchill would broadcast them, constantly pressing his guests for another round. With furtive glee, he would hand out stiff concoctions to visitors while diluting his own brandy or whisky from the seltzer siphon. Yet, despite the weak libations, Churchill seemed to reinforce the bibulous impression. Away from the public forum, his rhetorical guard was let down in conversation. His monologues on history or political issues became slathered with lisps and often shaken by a vehement stammer, which he could control in his rehearsed and prepared speeches.

Churchill undoubtedly drank a lot by today's more health-conscious standards, and social customs of the time do not excuse excess. Yet whatever his consumption, Churchill's years at Chartwell were marked by prodigious literary output. Despite his parliamentary responsibilities, he wrote weekly articles and columns, as well as his four-volume biography, *Marlborough*. When that was finished, he began his *History of the English-Speaking Peoples*.

But geniuses like Churchill are often considered suspect. Certainly his warnings

HAT TRICK

As a statesman, soldier, author, painter, bricklayer, horseman, and pilot, Churchill wore many hats—and not just figuratively. "Father never met a hat he didn't like," said Churchill's son Randolph. Indeed, Churchill wore and collected hundreds of hats, including a Native American war bonnet sent to him in honor of his Iroquois lineage on his mother's side.

When meeting Roosevelt, Churchill always donned his naval officer's blue peaked cap. For General Eisenhower, he switched to his army major's cap. When Churchill went to North Africa to meet both Eisenhower and Roosevelt, he wore a pith helmet. On his first meeting with Stalin in Moscow in 1942,

Left: Churchill wearing ceremonial garb in 1946. Center: A wide-brimmed fashion statement in 1949. Right: Sporting his everyday hat in 1948.

he greeted the dictator with a Russian bearskin. In Teheran the next year, meeting with FDR and Stalin, he sported a Turkish fez.

As Home Secretary in 1908, Churchill acquired a fire chief's helmet and a London "bobby's" headgear. While painting in the sun on the Riviera, he wore a sombrero sent to him from Cuba, although occasionally he donned a 10-gallon Texas Stetson. But for daily wear, he preferred a hybrid combination of homburg and bowler that Locke's of London made especially for him.

on Germany and a likely World War II just reinforced the impressions that he was an erratic and volatile man. Those in denial of his prophecies vented their displeasure on the prophet.

Better to trust Baldwin; the pipe-smoking prime minister was the quintessence of the stalwart Yorkshire farmer. Though strong in the public's affection, Baldwin was weak in health. He left 10 Downing Street in 1937, giving way to Neville Chamberlain. The new prime minister continued the appeasement policies of his predecessor, but he also embraced the anti-Communist views of the British establishment—including the Anglican Church, the London *Times,* and even the Crown. Many business leaders saw the Communists as a greater threat than the Fascists. To those people, Hitler was a responsible German nationalist fighting Communism, while Churchill was irresponsible in attacking the government.

In 1938, when Hitler annexed Austria, Churchill rose from his habitual corner seat in the House, head thrust forward, thumbs in vest pocket, and lectured the Conservative government on the years they had wasted:

"For five years I have talked to this House on these matters—not with very great success. I have watched this famous island descending incontinently, recklessly, the stairway which leads to a dark gulf. It is a fine broad stairway at the beginning, but after a bit, the carpet wears. A little further on there are only flagstones; and a little further on still, these break beneath your feet."

An embarrassed silence greeted Churchill as he ended. Then members, anxious to turn to more pleasant thoughts, rattled their papers and shuffled out to the lobby—many heading for tea. One member told his guest in the gallery, author Virginia Cowles: "It was the usual Churchill filibuster. He likes to rattle the saber and he does it jolly well, but you have to take it with a grain of salt."

After Austria, Hitler turned to Czechoslovakia. On the cranked-up charge that this Slavic nation was oppressing its sizable number of German-speaking residents, Hitler threatened to "rescue" them with troops. To calm a rattled Britain, Prime Minister Chamberlain pledged he would meet Hitler in Munich with the hope of bringing back peace.

In Churchill's mind, that was the equivalent of giving the Nazi dictator a blank check. When it came to Czechoslovakia, Churchill's own intelligence suggested that Hitler was bluffing with a weak hand. The Czech Army had a half million men in its fortified mountain strongholds. Furthermore, the French along the German border had three times the ground forces of the Germans. For those reasons, the German Army High Command was opposed to committing its troops to war over Czechoslovakia.

Yet Chamberlain went to Munich and agreed to dismember Czechoslovakia. He returned with a settlement proclaiming that he had achieved "peace with honour."

Massive crowds turned out in London to greet Chamberlain on his return. Chamberlain was acclaimed by King George and a grateful House of Commons as a savior. Amidst the cheers, Churchill made this private aside to a member of Parliament about Chamberlain: "He had the choice between war and dishonor. He chose dishonor, and he will get war anyway."

Peace at Any Price
The headlines screamed "Peace!" when Chamberlain returned from Munich—and barely mentioned the partitioning of another sovereign nation. Observed Churchill: "Silent, mournful Czechoslovakia recedes into the darkness."

THE MEN WHO NEVER MET

Hitler (at a Nazi Party rally in Buckeberg in 1934) possessed "the most virulent hatred that has ever corroded the human breast," said Churchill.

In a muddy Belgian trench in the spring of 1916, a corporal in the kaiser's army fidgeted and paced within the narrow confines. Not more than thirty yards away, across no-man's land, a cigar-smoking British major was inspecting trench defenses.

It was the closest Winston Churchill ever came to Adolf Hitler.

Sixteen years later, a meeting between the two men was actually set up. Churchill was near Munich, retracing the military maneuvers of the Duke of Marlborough for the biography of his ancestor. He met Ernest Hanfstaengl, an art publisher and close friend of Hitler. Hanfstaengl, a Harvard graduate with an American mother, had become Hitler's chief contact for promoting the Führer to the Americans and British. Hanfstaengl proposed a lunch at a Bavarian tavern. He told Churchill how much the British politician and Hitler had in common: two old soldiers who shared talents for painting and speaking. Churchill demurred, instead questioning Hanfstaengl on Hitler's views towards the Jews.

The meeting never came off.

AMBASSADOR KENNEDY

Churchill bids farewell to Ambassador Kennedy, whose removal he helped engineer, at 10 Downing Street in 1940.

The father of JFK was no favorite of Churchill's. In the late 1930s, Joseph Kennedy was ambassador to the Court of St. James, where he allied himself with those urging appeasement with Germany. He did not conceal his admiration for Hitler's revival of Germany, and often let slip some anti-Semitic views.

Franklin Roosevelt had sent Kennedy to London to get him out of Washington, where he was maneuvering against a Roosevelt third term in 1940. Roosevelt knew that Kennedy, the Irish-American social climber, would relish the appointment most sought after by old East Coast families.

In his reports to the president, Kennedy dismissed Britain's chances against Germany. At the time of Dunkirk in June 1940, Kennedy remarked that Britain was "down the tube." By then, Churchill had replaced Neville Chamberlain; as the new prime minister, he suggested to his friend Roosevelt that a new ambassador might be in order. Roosevelt replaced Kennedy with John Winant, a former governor of New Hampshire and chairman of the Social Security Board.

The next day, Churchill rose to tell the House:

"This is only the beginning of the reckoning. This is only the first foretaste of the bitter cup which will be proffered to year by year, unless by a supreme recovery of moral health and martial vigour, we rise again and take our stand for freedom as in the olden time." Churchill's was a lonely voice amid the rejoicing for peace. The cheers for Chamberlain the peacemaker, however, turned to deadly silence when Nazi troops marched into Prague the next spring.

The British were learning, to their dismay, that the desire for peace does not ensure peace. Three successive prime ministers had closed their eyes to the arming of Germany. After the pacifism of Ramsay MacDonald, the laissez-faire of Stanley Baldwin, and the appeasement of Neville Chamberlain, the day of reckoning had come. A price would have to be paid for those sleepy years and squandered opportunities.

War came on September 1, 1939, when German Panzer divisions rumbled past the Polish frontier in the early hours of a Sunday morning. A shaken Chamberlain government, desperate for unity, at least in his own party, asked its principal attacker to join the cabinet as first lord of the Admiralty.

For Churchill, the years in the wilderness had been strangely fruitful. Far from the corridors of power that had been darkened with dishonor, he had at last emerged in the eyes of his country with wisdom and respect. His detachment from ministries whose mediocrity would have only encumbered him had allowed the politician to become historian, orator, statesman, and prophet. He had chosen to await fate, and now it awarded him his hour.

To the ships at sea, the wire code was tapped out: "Winston is back."

Prelude to War

In April of 1939, with tension mounting in Europe, Churchill began criticizing Chamberlain's refusal to enact compulsory military service. Shortly thereafter, in Berlin, Germany's finance minister told a visiting British general that "Churchill is the only Englishman that Hitler is afraid of."

Britain
Alone
1939–1942

When Winston Churchill took his old desk at the Admiralty, it was a case of history repeating itself— not so much with a vengeance, but with a pardon. For here was Churchill, once more sitting in the same chair from which he had been so ignominiously dismissed after Gallipoli in 1915. Behind Churchill was the very same map of the North Sea on which he had then plotted the movements of the German fleet in World War I.

In the fall of 1939, the situation hardly qualified as a full-scale war. It was, as Churchill called it, the "Trance" or the "Twilight War." Others called it the "Phony War." On land, French troops stood poised behind the Maginot Line, as if in a catatonic standstill, while in the daylong dusk of the North and Baltic seas, the ships of Churchill's fleet passed in silent convoy through the Nazi-U-boat-infested waters.

As in World War I, Churchill was champing at the bit to do something that would immediately alter the course of the war. Then it was the Dardanelles. This time it would be Narvik. Germany was getting most of its steel from neutral Sweden, via the northern Norwegian port of Narvik. In a move to block the shipments, Churchill argued to the war cabinet for a landing at Narvik. In mid-April of 1940, a quickly assembled British expeditionary force was dispatched to the Norwegian coast. This time it was not the army that failed to assist the navy; it was the air force that never arrived to provide cover for the

Blitzkrieg
German soldiers pushed through the forests of Belgium in June of 1940, as Britons anxiously awaited their fate. "The day will come when the joybells will ring again throughout Europe," said Churchill.

Royal Marines. The British troops, fighting in impossible conditions, withdrew in defeat.

Yet thanks to the deployment of British mines and submarines, the operation did halt German shipping temporarily, Unfortunately, it also compelled Hitler to unleash the full force of Nazi might on Scandinavia, and Denmark and Norway were invaded.

In Britain, an outcry greeted the rout of the British landing force, with some critics labeling the affair "the second Gallipoli." But this time the blame was heaped on Prime Minister Chamberlain, not the first lord of the Admiralty.

Chamberlain was clearly in trouble. The invasion of Norway and Denmark ended the "phony" war, mocking Chamberlain's April 2 assertion that Hitler had "missed the bus," by not seizing his early military advantage. The "bus" had trampled down Denmark and Norway. Yet Churchill would have no part in any discussion of Chamberlain's failings. He remained loyal and dismissed any suggestions by political friends that he should succeed Chamberlain. Still, sentiment grew for a new prime minister. Compared to Winston's tough talk, Chamberlain had been sounding almost apologetic. On the day Britain declared war against Germany, he said:

"You can imagine what a bitter blow it was to me that my long struggle to win peace failed. Yet I cannot believe that there is anything different I could have done . . . we have a clear conscience."

Compare that to Churchill the same day:

"There is a generation of Britons here now ready to prove that it is not unworthy of those great men, the fathers of our land . . . We are fighting to save the world from a pestilence of Nazi tyranny and in defence of all that is most sacred to man…It is a war…to establish on impregnable rocks the right of the individual. It is a war to establish and revive the stature of man."

While Chamberlain was wringing his hands, Churchill was shaking his fist. To Chamberlain, war was a depressing duty, but to Churchill, it was the ultimate challenge. In his speech as first lord of the Admiralty in January 1940, Churchill had sounded the battle call in a series of short, sinewy phrases:

"Come then: let us to the task, to the battle, to the toil—each to our part, each to our station. Fill the armies, rule the air, pour out the munitions, strangle the U-boats, sweep the mines, plough the land, build the ships, guard the streets, succor the wounded, uplift the downcast, and honour the brave. Let us go forward together in all parts of the Empire, in all parts of the Island. There is not a week, nor a day, nor an hour to lose."

That was a leader's language—and in 1940, Britons were begging to be led. The defeat in Norway triggered a debate on Chamberlain's suitability as prime minister. On May 7, the veteran Conservative back-bencher Leo Amery hurled at the Chamberlain ministry the scornful words that Oliver Cromwell had once issued to the Long Parliament: "You have sat too long here for any good you have been doing. Depart, I say, and let us have done with you. In the name of God, go!"

Chamberlain's pitiable response was that his friends should not desert him, prompting the aging Lloyd George to reply, in the last great speech of his career:

"I say solemnly that the prime minister should give an example of sacrifice because I tell him that there is nothing which would contribute more to victory in this war than that he should sacrifice the seals of office."

While Hitler's Panzer divisions rolled their tanks and artillery in a wide swath of destruction into Holland and Belgium, Chamberlain called in Lord Halifax, the foreign secretary, and Churchill to discuss the prime minister question. Churchill neither supported Halifax nor advanced his own candidacy. He did, however, support the idea of a coalition government. Before one could be formed, Chamberlain resigned.

His decision paved the way for the king, in a rare use of his constitutional power, to name a successor.

"Britain's Warlord"
A week before Churchill became prime minister in 1940, *Life* magazine dubbed him "Britain's Warlord" (here, in a cover photo by Margaret Bourke-White). Time-Life boss Henry Luce was an early champion of Churchill.

LIFE

BRITAIN'S WARLORD

APRIL 29, 1940 10 CENTS

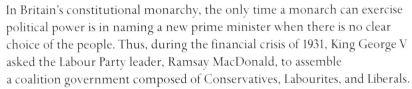

In Britain's constitutional monarchy, the only time a monarch can exercise political power is in naming a new prime minister when there is no clear choice of the people. Thus, during the financial crisis of 1931, King George V asked the Labour Party leader, Ramsay MacDonald, to assemble a coalition government composed of Conservatives, Labourites, and Liberals.

Now in 1940, the country needed a wartime coalition. The Conservative Party held the majority of seats, but with the resignation of Chamberlain, its new leader was Lord Halifax—an earl who sat in the House of Lords. Were he to be prime minister, members of the House of Commons would not be able to question him on the conduct of the war. The head of the Labour Party, Clement Attlee, objected to Halifax, as did the increasingly marginalized Liberal Party.

Favoring Churchill was Lloyd George, whose experience as Britain's leader during World War I carried much weight. King George VI now had to decide. The monarch had admired Chamberlain and privately considered Churchill a bit unstable. (George VI was known for his impeccably correct demeanor, and he never voiced those concerns outside the palace.) But he repressed his doubts and summoned Churchill to Buckingham Palace on May 10 to form a government.

Never had a prime minister assumed office in such a grave hour. The blitzkrieg was sweeping like a tornado across Europe. Each hourly newscast of the BBC reported the latest tidings of disaster from Holland, Belgium, and then France. Churchill's inaugural speech to the House of Commons was brief but brilliant, and it had an electric effect on the nation:

"I have nothing to offer but blood, toil, tears, and sweat . . . You ask, What is our policy? I will say: 'It is to wage war, by sea, land, and air, with all our might and with all the strength that God can give to us; to wage war against a monstrous tyranny, never surpassed in the dark, lamentable catalogue of human crime.' That is our policy."

The pent-up frustration from hundreds of days of impotence and indecision broke. In the House of Commons, grown men wept, not with despair but with relief. They took Churchill's promises of blood, sweat, and tears as if they were grants of nobility. If words of hope were all he had to offer, he gave them in rich measure. If the military arsenals of Britain were bare, the armory of its language was fierce.

On May 19, as French forces were reeling

Paris Falls

German troops march down the Champs-Elysées on June 14, 1940. Four days earlier, Churchill had flown to Paris and urged the French to defend their capital— but he was told that the citizens were already evacuating. Unlike Churchill, French General Weygand and Marshal Pétain had the mark of defeat on their faces.

from the German breakthrough at Sedan, Churchill called on the people of Nazi-occupied Europe to rally to the cause:

"Behind the armies and fleets of Britain and France gather a group of shattered states and bludgeoned races—the Czechs, the Poles, and Norwegians, the Danes, the Dutch, the Belgians—on all of whom the long night of barbarism will descend—unbroken even by a star of hope—unless we conquer, as conquer we must, as conquer we shall."

> "Look forward, do not look backward. Gather fresh in heart and spirit all the energies of our being, bend anew for a supreme effort."
>
> WINSTON CHURCHILL

Churchill knew his words might spell the difference between defeat and resistance. Any hesitation or faltering could mean collapse. All Europe now lay at Hitler's feet. On June 2, most of the British troops in France were trapped on the beach at Dunkirk. The English people—their will focused and their courage tapped—responded. A tide of English vessels moved across the Channel toward French beaches and British troops. Dories, dinghies, and skiffs swelled the ranks of the 860-boat flotilla in its rescue operation. While this "reverse armada" was taking place with its outcome shrouded in doubt, hurried councils organized by Lord Halifax at the British Foreign Office raised the possibility of negotiations with the Nazis.

By one report, Churchill came back to 10 Downing Street and remarked to a secretary: "What we need is another miracle, another Moses, someone to separate the English Channel as Moses did the Red Sea. The Germans, like the Egyptians, are right on top of our boys." In a sense, a "miracle" did occur: clouds descended low over the beaches and prevented the Luftwaffe from dispatching its aerial destruction on the boats filled with troops.

Churchill repaired that Sunday evening to the book-lined cabinet room at 10 Downing Street to prepare his remarks. On Tuesday he had to give his report on Dunkirk to the House of Commons. At the far side of the room, his secretary waited at her typewriter.

Reflectively, Churchill opened:

"We must be very careful not to assign to this deliverance the attributes of a victory . . . "

Then, pacing from the fireplace at the one end to the draped windows overlooking a garden at the other, Churchill dictated, first muttering under his breath snatches of words to himself, then in a burst of declamation, bellowing out the complete sentence in its full panoply. Sometimes when the echoed

CAVE PAINTINGS

On November 1, 1940, four boys searching for their lost dog in a cave at Lascaux, France, discovered a treasure of Paleolithic artwork—walls of a remote cave covered with vivid depictions of bison, wild horses, and cattle. The paintings, from 15,000–10,000 B.C., were clearly the work of skilled artists, and were probably meant to invoke magic that would ensure good hunting.

?

resonance of the dictated passage jarred Churchill's ear, he grumbled: "Gimme" and ratcheted the paper from the typewriter to scan the offending line.

By midnight the Churchill growl had faded to a croak:

"We shall go on to the end . . . Even though large tracts of Europe and many old and famous states have fallen or may fall into the grip of the Gestapo and all the odious apparatus of Nazi rule, we shall not flag or fail. We shall fight with growing confidence and strength in the air, we shall defend our island whatever the cost may be . . . "

He seemed, in the later words of his secretary, utterly spent by the effort. Then, with tremors shaking his voice, he declared in tones hardly above a whisper:

". . . we shall fight on the beaches, we shall fight on the landing grounds, we shall fight in the fields and in the streets, we shall fight in the hills…"

The words stopped. With his eyes moist from tears for his stricken country, Churchill grasped the back of a chair for a couple of silent minutes. Then, like the blare of a trumpet, he roared in deafening defiance:

". . . we shall never surrender!"

The Churchill phrases marched again:

". . . even if, which I do not for a moment believe, this island, or a large part of it, were subjugated and starving, then our empire beyond the seas . . . would carry on the struggle, until, in God's good time, the New World, with all its power and might, steps forth to the rescue and liberation of the Old."

The next day, on June 4, the prime minister delivered his address to an expectant House of Commons. The entire membership rose to a thunderous nine-minute ovation after the "We shall never surrender" charge. During the sustained roar of cheers, Churchill muttered on the side to the front bench: "And if they do land, we'll beat the bastards with the butt ends of broken beer bottles, which is bloody all we've got."

A Labour member of Parliament, Josiah Wedgwood, a scion of the pottery family, wrote " That was worth 1,000 guns, and the speeches of 1,000 years." Harold Nicolson, an English essayist and man of letters, was another parliamentarian who heard it. He wrote to his wife, the author Vita Sackville-West, that they were "the most magnificent words" ever uttered in the English language.

She wrote back:

"Even repeated by the announcer, it sent shivers down my spine. I think one of the reasons why one is stirred by his Elizabethan phrases is that one feels the whole massive backing of power and resolve behind them, like a great fortress: they are never words for words' sake"

From the House of Commons, Churchill went to the BBC studio at Shepherd's Bush to deliver the radio address. His speech would be carried to the Commonwealth nations of Canada, Australia, New Zealand, and the rest of the British Empire. But it was really targeted at one man—

New Job

At the end of his first day as prime minister, Churchill wrote: "I felt as if I were walking with destiny and that all my life had been preparation for this hour and for this trial."

Franklin Delano Roosevelt, president of the still-neutral United States.

In the residential quarters on the second floor of the White House, the president listened with his friend and principal aide, Harry Hopkins. When the speech was over, Roosevelt turned off the radio and said: "Well, Harry, if we give aid to England, it's not like the French—money down the rat hole. As long as that old bastard's in charge, Britain will never surrender."

With the fall of France, Britain was alone. From the Reichstag in Berlin, Hitler issued this directive on July 2, 1940: "The Führer and supreme commander has decided…that a landing in England is possible provided air superiority can be attained."

Churchill announced: "The Battle of France is over. The Battle of Britain is about to begin." That invasion, called Operation Sea Lion, was postponed until mid-September, when Hermann Göring boasted that an outnumbered and overwhelmed Royal Air Force would be wiped out. From the newly captured airfields in France, the bomber squadrons of the Luftwaffe and their fighter escorts raged across southern England. As high summer gave way to fall, the smoke from the wreckage of shot-down British planes darkened the British skies.

At the climax of the Battle of Britain on a September Sunday afternoon, Churchill drove with Clementine from the prime minister's country residence at Chequers to nearby Uxbridge, the underground nerve center of the Royal Air Force. On the wall was a map with red disks that would light up to indicate the placement position of the German Luftwaffe bombers and blue disks indicating the British Hurricane and Spitfire fighters. On the floor was a huge map showing the British and French coasts.

At about twilight, the prime minister, who was seated in the center of the first row, turned to the air chief marshal, Sir Charles Portal, and asked, "Where are the blue buttons? There are no more blue buttons lighting up."

The air marshal replied, "There are no more to be lit up—no more reserves. Every plane we have is now in the sky." Silence descended on the room. Of that crucial moment, Churchill wrote: "The odds were great; our margins small; the stakes infinite."

CHARLES DE GAULLE

Churchill understood that de Gaulle (in liberated Bayeux in 1944) was the leader that France would need after the war.

With a first name that evoked the memory of Charlemagne, and a surname that stood for France itself, it's little wonder that Charles de Gaulle believed leadership was his destiny. He was born in 1890 in Lille, the son of a philosophy teacher at a Jesuit college. A devout Catholic and top graduate of St. Cyr, the elite French military academy, the six-foot-four-inch de Gaulle was like a medieval knight sworn to the service of God and France. As leader of the Resistance, General de Gaulle demanded the deference and homage of a head of state. "De Gaulle seems to think he's Joan of Arc," remarked Churchill, "and the problem is my bishops won't allow me to burn him." Roosevelt despised de Gaulle, but Churchill, though irritated by his antics, actually admired him. And he knew the French needed a heroic figure to rally around.

After the war, de Gaulle served as prime minister, but soon quit. He returned in 1958 and ushered in a new constitution that called for a president with powers similar to those of the American chief executive. He resigned as president in 1969, and died the following year.

You never know who's listening!

CARELESS TALK
COSTS LIVES

The War at Home
This 1940 British propaganda poster depicted Hitler and an obese Hermann Goering eavesdropping on a conversation in the London Underground. The campaign sought to prevent the dispersal of military secrets that civilians might discover through their work on the war effort.

Some minutes later, a wing commander entered the room and began shutting off the lighted red disks on the wall. An emotional Churchill turned his thumbs up in a gesture of victory. Then with a broken voice, he uttered: "We've won! The Nazis are turning tail!"

He took from his pocket an envelope and scribbled these words in tribute to the young men who flew up to forty hours in the sky to beat the Germans back: "Never in the field of human conflict has so much been owed by so many to so few."

In the Blitz of London that followed, however, many more Britons would bear the weight of German wrath. Beginning in September, a Nazi air fleet of 1,000 planes began to bomb London's industrial East End and docks. When Churchill visited the damaged docks, the workers cried: "Good old Winnie. We knew you'd come and see us. We can take it. Now give it back." Churchill broke down and wept.

Because of the bombing threat, the British government persuaded a reluctant Churchill to move his command post from 10 Downing Street to an underground facility called the Annex, which was transformed into the Cabinet War Rooms. At the head of the table sat Churchill, in a homely wooden chair with rounded arms and a plump cushion. In front of him were four glass inkwells, two red and two black. Between the two pairs of inkstands was an ornamental dagger used as a letter opener. The dagger, Churchill told visitors, he was saving for his personal confrontation with Hitler. Just past the end of the ink blotter was a propped-up cardboard sign with the words of Queen Victoria:

"Please understand there is no pessimism in this house and we are not interested in the possibilities of defeat; they do not exist."

From this unlikely subterranean station, Churchill dispatched war directions by propelling hollow steel balls conveying messages through pneumatic pipelines to various government departments, with scarlet tags affixed to signal balls that contained actions to be carried out that very same day. As the Blitz began, the first order designated the London subway stations as bomb shelters. Then Churchill directed the House of Commons, which met during the bomb-filled night hours, to convene in the daytime at unscheduled sittings. The Local Defense Volunteers, who began the war as coastal watchers for invasion, were rechristened the Home Guard. For these men, often aged veterans of World War I, as well as for other gallant citizenry, Churchill instituted the George Cross award as the civilian equivalent of the Victoria Cross, which was given for bravery under fire. For the bombed-out homeless, he put through a national insurance plan for compensation.

THE CABINET WAR ROOMS

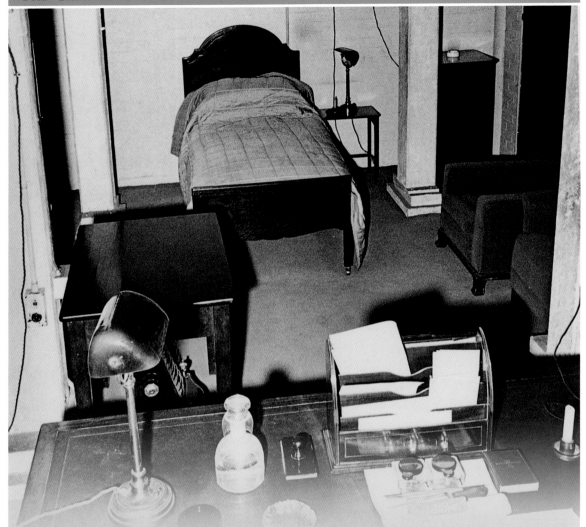

Churchill disliked this narrow bed in the Cabinet War Rooms, preferring the comfort of nearby 10 Downing Street. Nonetheless, he spent many nights here during the Blitz.

During World War II, the Cabinet War Rooms were located in a fortified basement on King Charles Street. The honeycomb of underground rooms, just a five-minute walk from 10 Downing Street, had been a storage facility for old documents. For Churchill, the bunker became his home away from home during the war—a sheltered place to work, sleep, and live for as long as necessary.

Churchill's combined office included a narrow bed that was superior to the cots offered to others, but it was still spartan. He did, however, have communications systems that were sophisticated for the day—including BBC microphones for live world broadcasts and a scrambled "hot line" telephone to President Roosevelt.

Churchill regularly inspected the Map Room, where large-scale maps of the Atlantic Ocean, the seas around the United Kingdom, and the Far Eastern theaters charted global war operations. Each day he would go over the plans, marking the advance of the Allies.

Today, the Cabinet War Rooms are a popular tourist attraction in London.

Hardly a detail escaped his attention. One October directive insisted on a sufficient candy and chocolate supply for children.

Yet the directives, minutes, and telegrams—which by the end of the war numbered over one million—were not as instrumental as the speeches he composed and delivered in the heroic months of London's siege. In a September radio speech entitled "Every Man to his Post," Churchill echoed the mood of all Britons:

"We shall...draw from the heart of suffering itself the means of inspiration and survival, and of a victory won not only for ourselves but for all..."

Borrowing from John Bunyan, the 17th-century preacher and author of *Pilgrim's Progress*, Churchill ended a summary of the war effort to the House of Commons with this intensely spiritual invocation:

"Long, dark months of trials and tribulations lie before us. Not only great dangers but many more misfortunes, many shortcomings, many mistakes, many disappointments will surely be our lot. Death and sorrow will be the companions of our journey; hardship our garment; constancy and valour our only shield. We must be united; we must be undaunted; we must be

Palace Takes a Hit
King George VI (in naval dress uniform) and his wife Elizabeth survey bomb damage to Buckingham Palace. Referring to the previous Nazi devastation of London's East End, Elizabeth said, "I can now look the East End in the face." The popular Elizabeth, later known as the Queen Mum, died in 2002 at the age of 102.

inflexible. Our qualities and deeds must burn and glow through the gloom of Europe until they become the veritable beacon of its salvation."

In his monastic underground quarters, Churchill, wearing his favorite green-dragoned dressing gown, dictated speeches while propped up by two pillows on the narrow bed. Sentences came between puffs of a pungent Havana cigar, whose clouds filled the small cell. At the table, a tense young secretary would punch out the words on her typewriter. There was no time to waste transcribing shorthand notes. Instead, the secretary would try to transpose his message into a rough first draft, triple-spaced to allow room for revisions by the perfectionist. The prime minister already had a rough outline in his head, which he had been mulling over days earlier—perhaps in strolls in the garden at 10 Downing Street or in the walks to and from the Annex to Downing Street. The workings of Churchill's mind can be seen in the notes he used for an emergency Commons speech in secret session, for which he did not have time to prepare a proper address:

We have had a couple of nights of bombing,
    evidently much worse than that.
Folly underrate gravity of attack impending.
But if 100 or 150 bombers employed
    entitled to remark:
    Not very cleverly employed.
Hardly paid expenses.
Learn to get used to it.
    Eels get used to skinning.
Steady continuous bombing,
    probably rising to great intensity
      occasionally,
        must be regular condition of our life.
        The utmost importance preserve morale of people,
        especially in the night work of factories
        A test of our nerve against theirs.
        …essence of defence of Britain
        is to attack the landed enemy at once,
        leap at his throat
        and keep the grip until the life is out of him.

This first draft reduced the inchoate musings in Churchill's head to paper. Back to the secretary it would go, sentences crossed out and replacements penned over them, and then various arrows pointing to additional paragraphs in the margin or perhaps reversing the order of certain sentences.

Even though this polishing extended to a third or even fourth draft, Churchill would continue revising the final copy up until

DEBUT OF THE JEEP

The U.S. Army Quartermaster Corps introduced the Jeep in late 1940. The Jeep was designed as a "general purpose" military vehicle—hence the name, which suggested the sound of "GP." Built by Willys, the Jeep's high clearance made it capable of negotiating rough terrain like bombed-out roads. It was used extensively in World War II as a command vehicle and small personnel carrier.

the very last minute before he left for the House of Commons, or when the BBC technicians entered the Annex to set up a broadcast from his cubicle. The last-minute changes exasperated a finicky Foreign Office, which insisted on their bureaucratic prerogative of approval.

The final copy, which was typed on a special octavo sheet, broke up the script into lines, as in verse. Frequently the margins held stage directions like "pause" or "emphasis." Churchill believed that rhetoric, with its appeal to the ear, should be spaced out like poetry, in order that it could be read like verse:

> We cannot yet see how deliverance will come
> or when it will come,
> But nothing is more certain
> than that every trace of Hitler's footsteps,
> Every stain of his infected
> and corroding fingers,
> Will be sponged and purged
> and, if need be, blasted
> from the surface of the earth.

Voice of the Beeb

Few in wartime Britain would have recognized his face, but just about everybody knew the voice of Richard Dimbleby, the BBC announcer who introduced Churchill when he made his radio addresses. Dimbleby's stately Oxford accent was almost as reassuring as the words of the prime minister during Britain's darkest hours.

Churchill's delivery was unique. Richard Dimbleby, "the voice of the BBC" who introduced Churchill's radio broadcasts, said the peculiarity of the Churchill inflection had the power to command rapt attention. It did not sound like the typical clipped accent of the London stage or the BBC. In the educated Oxonian of those professional speakers, the consonants are clear and the vowels are shortened.

But Churchill would do the opposite, muting the consonants and accenting the vowels. He had learned to disguise his lifelong lisp by making his "s," as well as all his consonants, weak. The vowels then stood out: "blOOd, swEAt, and tEArs"—one could hardly hear the "sw" in "sweat." Again, unlike the typical British inflection, the Churchill intonation would generally rise instead of fall to signal a completed thought or sentence.

Churchill also inserted a voluntary stammer as a prelude to a key word— developed as a way to overcome the anxiety caused him by his natural stutter. For example, Churchill described the Lend-Lease Act passed by Congress in 1941 in a word never used before in the English language: "it is a most (uh, oh, uh) unsordid deed."

Before Churchill ever became prime minister, he realized that only the president of the United States could wrest America from its course of neutrality. The wooing of Roosevelt began in 1939, when Churchill (as First lord of the Admiralty) had written his initial letter to the U.S. chief executive. The author had veiled the secret correspondence with the cryptic signature "Naval Person." The reference touched on a common bond between Churchill and Roosevelt, who had been assistant secretary of the navy in World War I.

He persuaded Roosevelt that a Britain which would never surrender would become the first line of U.S. defense. Although the U.S. Neutrality Act prevented the granting of military aid, the wily Roosevelt, citing an almost-forgotten statute on the books, had circumvented the act by leasing fifty destroyers to Britain.

The deployment of the aging destroyers proved mostly symbolic, as was the subsequent dispatch in January 1941 of Roosevelt's closest confidant, Harry Hopkins, as personal envoy to the British prime minister. Hopkins's message from the U.S. president consisted of words from the Book of Ruth: "Thy people shall be my people and thy God, my God, even to the end." On hearing it, a deeply moved Churchill turned his head away in tears.

Following in Hopkins's footsteps came Wendell Willkie, the recently defeated Republican presidential candidate, whose visit under Roosevelt's auspices signaled the mounting bipartisan sympathy for the British cause. Churchill, in a broadcast from the War Rooms, implored that the sympathy be undergirded by support:

"The other day, President Roosevelt gave his opponent in the late presidential election a letter of introduction to me, and in it he wrote out a verse, in his own handwriting, from Longfellow, which he said, 'applied to your people as it does to us.' Here is the verse:

Sail on, O Ship of State!
Sail on, O Union, strong and great!
Humanity with all its fears,
With all the hope of future years,
Is hanging breathless on thy fate!

"What is the answer that I shall give, in your name, to this great man, the thrice-chosen head of a nation of a hundred and thirty million? Here is the answer which I will give to President Roosevelt: Put your confidence in us. Give us your faith and your blessing, and under Providence, all will be well.

"We shall not fail or falter; we shall not weaken or tire. Neither the sudden shock of battle, nor the long-drawn trials of vigilance and exertion will wear us down. Give us the tools, and we will finish the job."

To a Congress that had just heard the outlines of the proposed Lend-Lease Act by Roosevelt, a bottom line had never been expressed more succinctly.

In the early months of 1941, when British troops were being driven out of the Balkans and Greece, the guarantee of military aid from the United States was the only good news to a bomb-ravaged Britain. At home, as the long nights of winter shortened into summer, the

Sail On
A scroll of Longfellow's famous verse of hope, recited to Churchill by FDR, was signed by both men after the Atlantic meeting. Longfellow was the first American poet to have a bust in the Poet's Corner at Westminster Abbey.

AIL ON, O SHIP OF STATE!
Sail on, O Union, strong and great!
Humanity with all its fears,
With all the hopes of future years,
Is hanging breathless on thy fate!

The Longfellow verse in Mr Roosevelt's Message to Mr Churchill.

whine of sirens and burst of shells, which for so many months had punctuated the hours of the London dark, became sporadic. By June, nothing heavier than a gentle English shower rained on the British rooftops. Soon the reason for the halt was clear: Hitler's interest had been diverted.

On June 21, while Churchill was weekending at Chequers (see page 108), the military staff telephoned him that German armored divisions were hurtling past the Polish frontier into the Soviet Union. Churchill was not surprised. Not only had he predicted the attack for the last couple of months, but he had also instructed his envoys to communicate that intelligence to a disbelieving Stalin. From the very outset, Churchill had been convinced that the 1939 deal between the two dictators to carve up Poland was a bond that would soon unravel from its own sleaziness.

On the Chequers lawn, Churchill, between puffs of his cigar, told John Colville, his parliamentary secretary: "Jock, we'll have to now send arms to Russia."

"How can you say that," countered Colville, "when you once said that the strangling of Bolshevism at birth would have been an untold blessing to the human race?"

Churchill replied: "If Hitler invaded the realms of Hell, I would find some way to make a favorable reference to the devil in the House of Commons."

The socialists in Churchill's coalition government were delighted with Churchill's call for aid to the Soviet Union. To some disgruntled Conservatives, Churchill gave his answer in the House of Commons:

"We have but one aim, and one single irrevocable purpose. We are resolved to destroy Hitler and every vestige of the Nazi regime. From this nothing will turn us—nothing. We will never parley; we will never negotiate with Hitler or any of his gang. We shall fight him by land; we shall fight him by sea; we shall fight him in the air, until, with God's help, we have rid the earth of his shadow and liberated its people from his yoke. Any man or state who fights on against Nazidom will have our aid. Any man or state who marches with Hitler is our foe."

Churchill believed that if the British and the Soviet people could hold out for the next four or five months, eventual victory was possible. For one

Atlantic Encounter
Roosevelt and Churchill forged a close relationship during their top-secret five-day meeting off the coast of Newfoundland in the summer of 1941. Here the two confer after Sunday services aboard the battleship *Prince of Wales* on August 10.

thing, believed Churchill: "The Russian Bear of a winter would hug Hitler's armies to death as it did Napoleon." So by July, British convoys were regularly sailing eastward to Soviet ports, carrying supplies Britain could barely spare from its own needs.

Then, in August, a different type of convoy ventured westward bearing a cargo even more vital—Churchill himself. The battleship *Prince of Wales* swept beside the president's ship, the *Augusta,* on the North Atlantic off Canada. The strains of "God Save the King" sounded from the U.S. Marine Band. Standing, with the support of his son, was Franklin Roosevelt, his hand raised in salute. Churchill emerged on deck in a peaked sailing cap and naval jacket. With a beaming smile, he said: "At long last, Mr. President, glad to see you aboard," to Roosevelt, clad in a white Palm Beach suit.

At the sea meeting, Churchill drafted, with a few later revisions by Roosevelt, the Atlantic Charter—a pledge of mutual support by both leaders for a world in which freedom and democracy would replace repression and tyranny. But even more than in the charter, Churchill found in the Sunday church service, held on the quarterdeck beneath the ship's guns, a tangible expression of their common purpose. As the sun broke through the mist that Sunday morning, the chorus of the old hymn "Onward, Christian Soldiers" rose to the sky in the mingled voices of two navies—"fighting men," as Churchill later retold to the House of Commons, "of the same language, of the same faith, of the same fundamental laws, of the same ideals, and now, to a larger extent, of the same interests, and certainly, in different degrees, facing the same danger."

On his homeward voyage, Churchill spied in the distance a vast flotilla of merchant ships—freighters, tankers, and converted passenger liners—on their way to England from America, carrying the desperately needed munitions and equipment. Churchill saw his chance to say "thank you" to the ships of the U.S. Merchant Marine. In the fading light of sunset, the *Prince of Wales* plunged ahead, cutting a lane through the six-column convoy at twenty-two knots. Not once but twice, the British battleship plowed through the motley steel ranks.

V FOR VICTORY

Churchill's victory sign (flashed here in 1949) became as famous as his face.

Churchill first raised his fingers in the famous V sign after it had been reported to him that in conquered Europe, Vs were being painted on walls at night by resistance forces—standing for *victoire* in French and *vrijheid* in Dutch. After being filmed in newsreels making the sign, Churchill started a national craze for everything V-related. The BBC began to incorporate the opening bars of Beethoven's Fifth Symphony to announce winning war news and patriotic programs, after it was noticed that the music's *duh-duh-duh-dahhhh* rhythm echoed the *dot-dot-dot-dash* symbol for V in Morse code.

Following the war, the sign became the symbol of Churchill himself. The V in one hand and a cigar in the other became as much a part of his appearance as a bow tie. Not surprisingly, the statue of Churchill by William McVey in front of the British Embassy in Washington depicts him in that familiar stance.

Standing on its bridge was the British prime minister, with his one hand in a V sign and the other raised in salute to the onlooking American Merchant Marine crews.

At the historic meeting, in which the charter was almost an afterthought, the two leaders and their advisors had discussed the emergence of Russia and Japan as crucial factors in the balance of power. Three months later, the Americans, as well as the British, were surprised by the Japanese.

Right-wing isolationists at the time would later charge that Churchill knew about the Japanese plans to bomb Pearl Harbor but held back an intelligence report from Roosevelt to ensnare the United States into the war. The fact is that the British Pacific Fleet in Singapore and Malaya was virtually wiped out. The tonnage of British ships sunk exceeded that of the American losses at Hawaii. For the only English statesman to be twice first lord of the Admiralty to destroy his own Pacific Fleet is unthinkable.

Furthermore, why would the Japanese bombing force the United States to make war against Germany? Hitler's folly of declaring war against the United States the day after Pearl Harbor could not have been predicted. Anyway, Roosevelt, a noted "Navy Firster," might have been guided by his naval chief of staff Ernest King—known for his anglophobia—to concentrate entirely on the Pacific. King, like all U.S. admirals, considered the Pacific "an American lake."

Finally, it is a wicked calumny to suggest that Churchill would deliberately send thousand of British and American sailors to their deaths. December 7, 1941, found Churchill and his two U.S. guests, Averell Harriman and Ambassador John Winant, were dining at Chequers. At 9:00 P.M., they tuned in to the BBC news. Immediately, Churchill telephoned Roosevelt.

"It's quite true," the U.S. president said. "They have attacked us at Pearl Harbor. We are all in the same boat now." Despite that shock, Churchill was almost joyous. He wrote later: "I went to bed and slept the sleep of the saved and thankful."

Day of Infamy

The American battleships *West Virginia* and *Tennessee* are engulfed in flames after the Japanese attack on Pearl Harbor. The Japanese aggression guaranteed America's entry into the war—and sealed the fate of the Axis powers.

Partnership Against Tyranny

1942–1945

The Japanese attack on Pearl Harbor compelled Churchill to go to Washington. If he did not, Churchill could envision the United States mobilizing all its energies on defeating Japan, leaving Britain and the Soviet Union to fend for themselves against Germany and Italy.

When Roosevelt asked Congress for a declaration of war, it applied only to Japan. But the day after Pearl Harbor, Hitler, with Mussolini following suit, declared war against the United States. The absurdity of this action has never been fully explained. But it gave Churchill all the more reason to sell Roosevelt on the necessity of defeating Germany as the number-one objective.

Suspecting Churchill's intentions, Roosevelt did not initially warm to the prime minister's plan to come to America. Churchill, however, insisted and prevailed. On December 12, he left on the battleship *Duke of York* for America. Ten days later, he arrived in Washington and was welcomed by the Roosevelts into the White House, where he was invited to light the Christmas tree. It was his first Christmas away from Clementine and his family. While he worked on Christmas Eve in the Monroe Room, polishing his speech to Congress for December 26, he asked the White House to send Diana Hopkins, who with her father lived in the White House, to come around to his room. A very nervous nine-year-old was ushered into the prime minister's presence. In his green robe, he held out his arms and embraced the awestruck

FRANKLIN D. ROOSEVELT

Churchill once said of Franklin Roosevelt: "Meeting him was like opening your first bottle of champagne." Indeed, the wartime intimacy between the two heads of state has never been equaled. On one occasion, Roosevelt wheelchaired himself into the Monroe Bedroom in the White House, where Churchill was staying. He was greeted by the pink-skinned prime

At their January 1943 meeting in Casablanca (above), Roosevelt and Churchill agreed to accept nothing less than unconditional surrender from the Axis powers.

minister just emerging from the bath. Roosevelt reversed his wheels for a quick exit. Churchill yelled out, "Pray do not leave. The king's first minister has nothing to hide from the president of the United States."

Diana, saying: "I'm a lonely old father and grandfather on Christmas Eve, and I wanted a little girl to hug."

He also needed to embrace Congress. Churchill's speech at the U.S. Capitol would be every bit as important, if not more so, than his opening address as prime minister. Washington's proprietary feelings for the Pacific Ocean had been shattered now by the sudden jeopardy of the Philippines, the Aleutians, and Hawaii. Congress might well resist the Churchill plan to concentrate first on Germany.

Concentration was not so easy for Churchill at the White House, amid festivities on Christmas Day. Harry Hopkins, who had the suite next door, as well as the president, kept popping in for chats, which often evolved into deep discussions of war strategy. Churchill wanted to convey something of the same intimacy in his rhetorical message to Congress the next day. He opened his speech with an allusion to both his mother and his Revolutionary War ancestry:

"Members of the Senate and the House of Representatives…the fact that my American forebears have for so many generations played their part in the life of the United States and that here I am, an Englishman, welcomed into your midst makes this experience one of the most moving and thrilling of my life.

"I wish indeed that my mother, whose memory I cherish across the veil of years, could have been here to see me. By the way, I cannot help reflecting that if my father had been American and my mother British, instead of the other way around, I might have got here on my own. In that case, this would not be the first time you have heard my voice."

At this deft speculation of what could have been his future in American politics, laughter rolled up toward him from the representatives and senators. He was no longer a foreigner, a visiting head of state, but one of them, a politician with kindred roots and ties. Then, with the audience firmly in his hand, Churchill guided them around the globe in a general survey of the war situation. When he came to Japan, a silence tense with anticipation gripped his listeners:

"After the outrages they have committed upon us at Pearl Harbor, in the Pacific Islands, in the Philippines, in Malaya and the Dutch East Indies, they must know that the stakes for which they have decided to play are mortal. When we look at the resources of the United States and the British Empire compared to those of Japan, it becomes…difficult to reconcile Japanese action with prudence or even sanity."

Then, gripping his lapels, he squared his shoulders and asked the rhetorical question:

"What kind of a people do they think we are?"

The audience roared its reply, as the members rose to their feet and thunderously cheered. For minutes, waves of applause flooded the chamber in a demonstration unparalleled in Capitol history.

Congressional Mettle
Churchill's December 26, 1941, address to Congress may well have been the greatest speech of his life. His insolent defiance of Japanese and German aggression, broadcast on national radio, helped rally Americans to the cause.

> "The United States is like a gigantic boiler. Once the fire is lit under it, there is no limit to the power it can generate."
>
> WINSTON CHURCHILL

White House Guest

Churchill models his "siren suit" at the White House on January 3, 1942, with Roosevelt aide Harry Hopkins, Hopkins's daughter Diana, and the president's Scottie dog, Fala. Churchill dubbed Hopkins "Lord Root of the Matter" for his ability to quickly solve problems.

"Is it possible [Churchill continued when the uproar subsided] that they do not realize that we shall never cease to persevere against them until they have been taught a lesson which they and the world will never forget?"

Then, shifting into a lofty theme for his peroration, Churchill raised again the Atlantic Charter concept of a postwar organization for keeping peace:

"Duty and prudence alike command…that the germ centers of hatred and revenge shall be constantly and vigilantly curbed and bested in good time and that an adequate organization should be set up to make sure that the pestilence can be controlled at its earliest beginning before it spreads and rages throughout the entire earth . . . "

Then he said, in closing:

"It is not given to us to peer into the mysteries of the future. Still I avow my hope and faith, sure and inviolate, that in the days to come the British and American people will for their own safety and for the good of all walk together in majesty, in justice, and in peace."

At the end, Churchill stood still for a moment at the rostrum and then sat down. For an instant, there was silence. Then pandemonium broke loose. Senators, representatives, cabinet secretaries, and Supreme Court justices cheered and waved, some of them exchanging V signs with the British prime minister. Beneath the bare cherubic forehead, the apple-cheeked face of Churchill beamed, basking in the tumultuous response. Churchill, the personification of John Bull, had won the heart of Congress. On returning to the White House, he told his bodyguard Walter Thompson: "I really hit the target." The speech had evoked the greatest reception in his long career.

But the effort took its toll. That night, while trying to open a window in his White House bedroom, Churchill felt a sudden pain in his chest. It was a mild heart attack. Fearing that publicity of the attack would compromise Allied morale, Churchill's doctor concealed it from the world; not even Churchill knew.

Disobeying his doctor's orders, Churchill did not rest for even a day. There was too much work to do. He left his bed to continue discussions with General Marshall and Admiral King, solidifying the Churchill-Roosevelt decision to make the defeat of Germany the first priority.

Then, again flouting medical warnings, he boarded a train for Ottawa to address the Canadian Parliament. After extolling the contribution of Canadian soldiers and fliers to the defense of Britain, Churchill identified all English-speaking peoples with their cousins in besieged Britain:

"I should like to point out to you that we have not at any time asked for any mitigation in the fury or malice of the enemy. The peoples of the British Empire may love peace. They do not seek the lands or wealth of any country, but they are a tough and hardy lot. We have not journeyed all this way across the centuries, across the oceans, across the mountains, across the prairies, because we are made of sugar candy.

"Look at the Londoners, the Cockneys; look at what they have stood up to. Grim and gay with their cry 'We can take it,' and their wartime mood of 'What is good enough for anybody is good enough for us.' We have not asked that the rules of the game should be modified. We shall never descend to the German and Japanese level, but if anybody likes to play rough we can play rough too."

Then, in the language of a Biblical prophet, he thundered a fateful judgment: "Hitler and his Nazi gang have sown the wind; let them reap the whirlwind."

Shifting tones, Churchill went on:

"When I warned [the French] that Britain would fight on alone, whatever they did, their generals told their prime minister and his divided cabinet: 'In three weeks England will have its neck wrung like a chicken.' "

Churchill paused and then hurled back the words: "Some chicken!"

Before he could finish, the Canadians were on their feet cheering. As the din lessened, Churchill added: "Some neck!" The uproar doubled again amid gales of laughter.

Journeying back to Washington, Churchill celebrated New Year's Eve on the train. As they neared Brattleboro, Vermont, he strode from his compartment to the dining car, armed with cigar and brandy. To the carful of reporters and staff aides, he gave a toast: "Here's to 1942. A year of toil, a year of struggle, a year of peril. But a long step toward victory."

But the year 1942 was almost over before the first "long step" was recorded—victory in North Africa, which for the British was the turning point of the war. To plan that campaign, Churchill returned to America in

No Time to Lose

This popular British propaganda poster was actually made just before Churchill became prime minister. The phrase was taken from a January 1940 speech he gave as first lord of the Admiralty: "Let us go forward together in all parts of the empire, in all parts of the island. There is not a week, nor a day, nor an hour to lose."

MONTY

British General Bernard "Monty" Montgomery gained fame with his victory over Field Marshal Rommel's Afrika Corps in 1942. Monty had bested Germany's finest general, and the bantam-sized British military leader in his red beret strutted like a rooster in his triumph.

To Eisenhower, the Irish-born Montgomery was like General George McClellan in the American Civil War—adored by his men but reluctant to commit his troops head-on because he was always overestimating the enemy's capability. Eisenhower told Churchill of his problems with Montgomery. "Ah, Monty," said the prime minister. "In defeat indomitable, in advance invincible," and then, after a puff of his cigar, "and in victory insufferable."

British General Montgomery (in North Africa) loved tanks as much as his U. S. counterpart, George Patton. His American commander, General Eisenhower, tolerated the cocky Brit because he knew the British troops adored him.

After the war, Montgomery advanced to the House of Lords, becoming Viscount of Alamein in 1948. At dinner in the House of Lords following his investiture, he saw Churchill in the Lords' lavatory. (Churchill had been having dinner in one of Lords' dining rooms.) "Why are you here, Winston? This is not the House of Commons. This is reserved for peers." Churchill replied, "Monty, in this porcelain chamber, aren't we all peers?"

Montgomery died in 1976, at age 89.

the summer, meeting with Roosevelt again. Later he journeyed to Cairo and met with the top military brass of both countries. Under the plan, U.S. General Eisenhower would take top command, with British General Bernard "Monty" Montgomery and American General George Patton fighting the German armies in a two-pronged attack.

While orchestrating these battle strategies, Churchill kept one eye on the longterm ramifications of the war. One night in London, after a long dinner, Churchill buttonholed Harold Macmillan and said, "Harold, we don't want to make Oliver Cromwell's mistake."

"What's that, Prime Minister?"

"He was so obsessed with Spain that he neglected the danger of France." As Macmillan later observed, Churchill was already foreseeing postwar problems with Britain's wartime ally, the Soviet Union. At a time when the Allies had not yet claimed a single victory in the war against Hitler, Churchill's ability to focus on that seemingly far-off problem struck Macmillan as remarkable.

In November 1942, Monty's victory over Field Marshal Rommel at El Alamein cheered the Allies. At the Lord Mayor's Luncheon, Churchill said:

"I have never promised anything but blood, tears, toil, and sweat. Now, however, we have a new experience. We have victory—a remarkable and definite victory. The bright gleam has caught the helmets of our soldiers, and warmed and cheered all our hearts…

"Now this is not the end. It is not even the beginning of the end. But it is, perhaps, the end of the beginning."

Churchill wrote later: "Before Alamein, we had no victories and afterwards hardly any losses."

In 1943, Allied tanks rolled across the Sahara sands to chase the retreating Rommel's armies out of Africa. For the rest of the year, the target was Italy. Churchill insisted on the invasion of Italy because a campaign there could lead, in his phrase, to "the soft under belly of the Axis." For one thing, Churchill hoped to free the Balkans before the Soviet armies reached them. On July 9, 1943, landings took place along the Sicilian coast. A month later, British tanks and American troops entered Palermo.

Victory in the Desert
A German panzer crewman surrenders to Montgomery's infantry soldiers during the battle at El Alamein, Egypt. The Allied victory triggered the German retreat from Africa, and set the stage for British and American troops to regain Western Europe.

As Montgomery and Patton maneuvered their tank divisions through Sicily in August of 1943, Churchill flew to Quebec to discuss with Roosevelt the imminent fall of Mussolini and plans for a Second Front. From Canada, Churchill trained to Boston for the presentation of an honorary degree by Harvard University. Churchill, in his majestically flowing robes of scarlet, reached the climax of his address on Anglo-American unity:

"Twice in my lifetime the long arm of destiny has reached across the ocean and involved the entire life and manhood of the United States in a deadly struggle . . .

"The price of greatness is responsibility . . . one cannot rise to be in many ways the leading community in the civilized world without being involved in its problems, without being convulsed by its agonies and inspired by its causes . . .

"The people of the United States cannot escape world responsibility . . . We have now reached a point in the journey where . . . it must be world anarchy or world order."

Tough Lady

First Lady and diplomat Eleanor Roosevelt (on her 66th birthday in 1950) respected Churchill but disagreed with his world view, which she felt promoted colonialism over the self-determination of new countries. In 1946 she denounced his Iron Curtain speech.

Then Churchill, after tracing the interwoven history, culture, and ideals of both countries, delivered his breathtaking proposal:

"This gift of a common tongue is a priceless inheritance, and it may well some day become the foundation of a common citizenship . . ."

From Boston, Churchill went to Hyde Park, New York, where Roosevelt drove Churchill around his Hudson River estate. Squire Roosevelt observed proudly: "You know, Winston, my Dutch ancestors were among the very first settlers here."

Churchill, whose American grandmother claimed to be one-eighth Iroquois, retorted: "But, Franklin, it was my ancestors who greeted them."

If FDR relished the banter of Churchill, his wife disapproved of the drinking, and the conversation that kept her weakened husband up until late at night. Eleanor also took issue with Churchill's colonialist views on India.

"The Indians," Mrs. Roosevelt charged, "have suffered for years under British oppression."

Churchill replied: "Well, Mrs. R., are we talking about the brown-skinned Indians in India who have multiplied under benevolent British rule, or are we speaking about the red-skinned Indians in America who, I understand, are now almost extinct?"

Eleanor, however, liked Clementine Churchill. She did not disagree when Mrs. Churchill said that she thought her husband's speech at Harvard about the idea of common citizenship was one of his greatest.

From Hyde Park, Churchill traveled to Washington. The American president and Mrs. Roosevelt, who were still vacationing at Hyde Park, had told Winston and Clementine in their absence "to treat the White House as their own home and to feel free to invite anyone to meals." To Churchill, his use of the White House and the occasion of his chairing the military conference in the Cabinet Room was "an event in Anglo-American history." The arrangement may have been Roosevelt's symbolic assent to the Churchill idea at Harvard.

In September, Churchill said of the threatened Mussolini: "That tattered lackey at Hitler's tail was now a whipped jackal frisking at the side of the German tiger." Indeed, as Allied armies advanced north in Italy, Hitler's troops had rescued *il Duce* from Rome and set him up as puppet head of a Nazi satellite "republic" in northern Italy. On September 8, 1943, Italy surrendered.

In November, Churchill flew to Teheran to meet with Roosevelt and Stalin. The Russian premier had only contempt for the Italian operation and threatened reprisals if the Allies tried to move eastward from Italy to the Balkans. Stalin also insisted to the Allied leaders that Poland should be under his power.

Most of all, Stalin demanded that the "Second Front"—the invasion of France—should begin immediately. Churchill and Roosevelt promised that an invasion across the English Channel would take place at the latest next spring, but the Stalin tirades muted the celebration of Churchill's sixty-ninth birthday party on November 30.

After Teheran, Churchill flew to General Eisenhower's command post in Algiers on December 10. As Eisenhower ushered him into his armored Cadillac, Churchill said in a tremulous voice: "Ike, I'm afraid I'll have to stay with you longer than I expected. I'm at the end of my tether." That night, Churchill was felled by pneumonia. A stroke followed the next day. His doctor fretted that he might die. Churchill, from his bedside, flashed a V sign and said: "Don't worry, Ike, if I die. The war is won."

Ike gave Churchill some his Zane Grey westerns to read for escape. And for the second consecutive Christmas, Churchill was away from London; but he recovered enough to leave his bed and sit down with Ike for a holiday turkey dinner in Algiers before returning to London for the New Year.

Eisenhower also went to London, and Churchill was seeing him regularly for a midweek luncheon at 10 Downing Street and a Friday-night dinner at Chequers. One time at Chequers, Churchill shook his head as Eisenhower briefed him on the latest plans for the cross-Channel invasion. "I have my doubts, Ike, when

STALIN

The five-foot-two-inch Stalin (with Churchill at Yalta in February 1945) wore platform heels when meeting with the British leader.

Churchill first met Russia's ruthless dictator in August 1942. Joseph Stalin, a little over five feet in stature with a sallow and pockmarked face and bad hygiene, did not make a good impression—particularly when he taunted Churchill by saying, "You British are afraid of fighting." Churchill managed to restrain himself, although he knew from intelligence reports that Stalin, on hearing the news of the German invasion, hid cowering under his desk.

Stalin was 44 years old in 1924, when he began seizing power after the death of Vladimir Lenin—largely by executing or exiling all his opponents. Until his own death in 1953, he oversaw the extermination of millions of his countrymen. (The next Soviet leader, Nikita Khrushchev, condemned Stalin and had his body removed from Lenin's tomb.)

Unlike FDR, Churchill never romanticized Stalin as "good old Uncle Joe." Churchill always knew he was dealing with a cruel tyrant. That was confirmed in Yalta when, in a private meeting with Stalin, Churchill observed a Russian note taker writing down his remarks. Churchill questioned Stalin about it; the next day Stalin told Churchill, "Don't worry. I've destroyed the notes, and the note taker."

CHEQUERS

Chequers is the country home of the British prime minister, like Camp David for the American president. The 40-room brick house was named by its original 16th-century owner, who worked at the Exchequer. The home was given to the government in 1921 by its then-owner, Lord Lee of Fareham.

It was at Chequers that Churchill heard on the radio the invasion of Russia by Germany in 1941, and later that year the news of Pearl Harbor. The room Churchill slept in is now called The Churchill Bedroom. In that room, Pamela Churchill (later Harriman) gave birth to his first grandson, Winston, in 1941. He used that bedroom as a study and office, and there he delivered some of his speeches, including the one addressed to America—"Give us the tools, and we will finish the job."

President Dwight Eisenhower (left) and Harold Macmillan, the prime minister of England, stroll the manicured lawn at Chequers. Churchill first visited Chequers in 1922, as a guest of David Lloyd George, then prime minister.

During the war, Churchill hosted General Eisenhower at Chequers every Friday night. Eisenhower called it "his sun lamp treatment," with Churchill reciting verses of Shakespeare, recounting the battle strategies of Wellington, or demonstrating a bayonet drill. After dinner a film would be shown. Churchill's favorite was Lawrence Olivier's version of *Henry V.*

On his last weekend in 1945, Churchill wrote in the guest book, "Finis." Yet the defeated prime minister would come back to Chequers in 1951.

I think of the beaches of Normandy choked with the flower of American and British youth, and when, in my mind's eye, I see the tides running red with their blood." Churchill took a puff of his cigar and blew it toward the ceiling and repeated: "I have my doubts, Ike, I have my doubts."

As plans for the invasion force were put into place, Churchill regularly questioned the logistical presentations made by the Allied army and navy heads. Once in a briefing, a British general made a projection of casualties saying, "A loss, I'd say, at 4,000 or so bodies." An angry Churchill broke in: "Sir, you will not refer to personnel of His Majesty's Forces as 'bodies.' They are live men. I will hear no more of that word!"

Churchill's mood varied from upbeat to downcast. On one moody occasion, he mused to Ike: "There is only one thing worse than trying to wage a war with allies."

"What's that?" asked Eisenhower.

"Trying to wage a war without them."

At a luncheon at 10 Downing Street, a worried Churchill confided to Eisenhower: "General, it's good for commanders to be optimistic, else they would never win a battle. But I must say to you, if by the time the snow flies, you have established your armies in Brittany on the Normandy coast and have the port of Cherbourg firmly in your grasp, I will be the first to congratulate a wonderfully conducted military campaign."

Then Churchill took another puff of his cigar and added: "If, in addition, you should have seized the port of Le Havre and all the area including the Cotentin Peninsula and the mouth of the Seine, I will proclaim that this is one of the finest operations in modern war."

"And finally," expanded Churchill, "if by Christmas you have succeeded in liberating the City of Light, our beloved Paris—if she can by that time regain her life of freedom and take her accustomed place as a center of Western European culture and beauty, then I will proclaim that this operation is the most grandly conceived and best conducted campaign known to the history of warfare."

To this Eisenhower replied: "Mr. Prime Minister, we expect to be on the borders of Germany by Christmas, pounding away at her defenses. When that occurs, if Hitler has the slightest judgment or wisdom left, he will surrender unconditionally to avoid complete destruction of Germany." Ike smiled. "Because of this conviction,

Message for Hitler
While visiting the front in Germany in 1945, Churchill chalked a personal greeting to Hitler—whom he called "Colonel Shicklgruber"— on a missile about to be fired into a German position.

ROCKET FIRE

Four days after the Allies landed at Normandy, Hitler began firing V-1 "Vengeance" rockets at London, from a base on the Baltic Sea. These first unmanned jet-powered weapons traveled at 370 miles per hour and carried one ton of explosives. Later in the year, the Germans unveiled the even deadlier V-2, which reached the speed of sound. German rockets killed thousands of Londoners before the war ended.

I made a bet with General Montgomery some months ago. The proposition was that we would end the war in Europe by the end of 1944. The bet was for £5, and I have no reason to want to hedge that bet."

The prime minister's face curved upward into a splendid smile. "My dear general, I pray you are right."

On May 15, Churchill invited the king to attend a conference with him at St. Paul's School in London. There Field Marshal Montgomery, an "Old St. Paulie," had made part of his former private school (which adjoins St. Paul's Cathedral) into a planning headquarters.

In the school's largest lecture room, armchairs were designated on the platform for the king, the prime minister, and General Eisenhower. The others sat on hard school benches. On the back of the platform, a map of the northern coast of France was displayed, marked with successive phase lines of the expected advances, day by day.

After a series of briefings, the prime minister then rose. Clad in black frock coat and striped trousers for his later attendance in the House of Commons, Churchill gestured with a huge Havana cigar as he spoke. His audience, which listened intently, was aware of his doubts about the cross-Channel invasion. Churchill, however, closed his remarks by grasping the lapels of his coat. "Gentlemen," he rasped, "I am now hardening to this enterprise."

In fact, he was so caught up in the landing plans that he told Eisenhower he wanted to go, too. It was a headache for Eisenhower. He told Mrs. Churchill, who then visited the queen at Buckingham Palace, and the two hatched a plan. A day later, King George VI called Churchill. In his habitual stutter, he said: "D-d-did you hear, Winston? It's j-j-jolly good news. I'm g-going with you on an invasion boat." Churchill, who would never risk the sovereign's life, realized he had been outflanked.

On June 6, 1944, the House of Commons—tense in the eerie government silence amid rampant rumors about landings in France—awaited the arrival of the prime minister. An unusually serene and reflective Churchill walked to his place at the front bench. In an offhand manner that toyed with the anxieties of the House, he opened with an announcement that was not news:

"The House should, I think, take formal cognizance of the liberation of Rome by the Allied Armies under the command of General Alexander, with General [Mark] Clark . . . This is a memorable and glorious event, which rewards the intense fighting of the last five months in Italy. The original landing . . . "

On Churchill droned, for several minutes, about the Italian situation as the chamber grew restless with more than the usual coughs and rustles of paper.

Then, almost casually, he shifted to a new topic.

"I have also to announce to the House that during the night and the early hours of this morning, an immense armada of upwards of 4,000 ships, together with several thousand smaller craft, crossed the Channel..."

A month later, Churchill was visiting Utah Beach in a British torpedo boat. At night, a sing-along in a British officers' mess hall erupted with a chorus of "Rule, Brittania." Churchill asked the officers if they knew the words of the second verse. He gave it to them:

MOUNTBATTEN

Born in 1900, Louis "Dickie" Mountbatten might well have been England's most glamorous figure of the 20th century. Handsome, brave, and gallantly charming, he looked as if he should have been king instead of his cousin George VI. Instead, he pushed forward his nephew Philip to be the husband of the future Queen Elizabeth II, and then became a second father for Prince Charles.

Churchill knew Mountbatten as a young man. He had appointed his father, Louis Battenberg, second sea lord in 1914 (Battenberg changed his name to Mountbatten due to anti-German sentiment.) In the 1930s, Dickie—unlike all other members of the royal family—agreed with the anti-appeasement views of Churchill.

Lord Mountbatten (reviewing Indian army units in New Delhi) admired the valor of colonial soldiers, who fought bravely in the Far Eastern theater of the war.

During the war, Churchill picked Mountbatten to lead a small cross-Channel invasion of France at Dieppe in 1942. The lightning raid suffered heavy casualties but gave the Allies needed experience for the later Normandy invasion. Churchill then made Mountbatten the head of British war operations in Asia against the Japanese. Churchill called Mountbatten his "triphibian" leader—"equally capable on land, sea, and air."

In 1979 the Irish Republican Army blew up Mountbatten's yacht, assassinating him because of his royal connections.

The nations, not so blest as thee,
Must in their turn, to tyrants fall,
While thou shalt flourish, great and free,
The dread and envy of them all.

On November 11, the anniversary of World War I's end, Churchill was at the Hôtel de Ville in Paris, the same city where the armistice was announced twenty-six years earlier. In response to a presentation by Charles de Gaulle, who had just marched in the Liberation Procession with him down the Champs-Élysées, Churchill said: "It gave me so much pleasure to see Paris again—this Paris which is a brilliant star shining above the world."

That same fall, a knockout blow against Japan was being planned. To bring Japan to its knees as soon as possible after Germany's defeat, Roosevelt had been telling Churchill that Russia must be persuaded to intervene in the Far East war. And the future world peacekeeping organization that had been discussed at Dumbarton Oaks, near Washington, said Roosevelt, must also have the Soviet Union's participation. Here were two vital reasons for another meeting with Stalin. Since FDR was fully occupied with his fourth presidential election, Churchill flew off without him to see "Uncle Joe," arriving in Moscow on October 9, 1944.

Despite his revulsion of international communism, Churchill managed to get on well with Stalin, unlike his British colleagues. He had no objections to Russian feasts and late nights, since he liked to keep midnight hours himself. And the Russians, on their part, were awed how this man now approaching his seventh decade could seemingly drink much younger men under the table.

By the first week in 1945, the German army was in retreat. They had

VE Day
Thousands throng before Buckingham Palace on May 8, 1945, where Churchill appeared on a balcony with the king and queen to acknowledge the end of the European theatre of war. After lunch with the royal family, Churchill went to the Ministry of Health and gave a speech.

spent their last reserves in a desperate offensive thrust in Belgium and Luxembourg—the Battle of the Bulge—and were now being driven east toward the Rhine.

With victory approaching, the Allied leaders agreed to meet in February at the Crimean resort of Yalta to seal plans for a new world organization, later to be called the United Nations. There it became clear to Churchill that his friend Franklin Roosevelt was approaching the end of his life.

The conference at Yalta was scheduled to last six days, which Churchill considered rather too few. "Even the Almighty took seven," he wrote to FDR. Preliminaries were then essential, and he arranged to meet the president first at Malta in the Mediterranean. Roosevelt received a cheerful ditty from his British friend on New Year's Day: "No more let us falter! From Malta to Yalta! Let nobody alter!" Nobody did; and the "Big Two" and their staffs duly arrived in Malta.

From Malta they flew to the Crimea. Churchill now noted how frail FDR looked. Churchill's doctor, Lord Moran, chose even more ominous words to describe the president: "Muffled in his cape, he looked old and thin and drawn…shrunken." Churchill described Roosevelt's failing powers differently: "His face had an air of purification and his eyes a faraway look."

Despite Churchill's fears, the U.S. president took Stalin at his word when the Soviet premier promised free elections in Poland. Because Soviet troops were already in that country, Churchill believed that only through a concerted action by the Americans and British could a Soviet takeover of Poland be averted. Churchill later said that Roosevelt at Yalta "maintained a slender contact with life and had no energy for disputes." FDR maintained that an implosion in the British Empire was a greater threat to another war than any Soviet aggressive actions.

A few days later in London, Churchill told the exiled President Benes of Czechoslovakia: "A small lion was walking between a huge Russian bear and a great American elephant, but perhaps it would prove to be the lion who knew the way."

On April 12, FDR telegraphed Churchill: "I would minimize the Soviet problem as much as possible." Early the next day, Churchill heard of the president's death in Warm Springs, Georgia. "I felt as if I had been struck a physical blow."

On the last day of April, another death shortened the struggle that had so exhausted the American leader. Adolf Hitler, in his underground bunker, had aimed a Walther pistol into his mouth.

A week later was VE Day—victory in Europe. A triumphant Churchill looked out from the balcony of the Ministry of Health building at the sea of faces that bobbed up and down in the joyous pandemonium.

"God bless you all," Churchill shouted in the microphone above the din. "This is your victory!"

"No, it is *yours*," the crowd yelled back. "It's yours."

"This is your victory!"
In his famous May 8 victory speech, Churchill said, "The evil-doers are now prostrate before us." But he reminded his countrymen that "Japan, with all its treachery and greed, remains unsubdued." He ended with the invocation "Advance, Britannia!"

Champion
of Freedom
1945–1951

After VE Day, the wartime coalition was dissolved, and a British general election had to be held. The results on polling day were delayed due to the counting of mailed-in military votes. Churchill nervously awaited returns in Potsdam, the Berlin suburb on the Havel River, where he was attending the "Big Three" meeting. There Churchill met President Truman for the first time. He was impressed by Truman's common sense and matter-of-fact style. The new American president also revealed to him the news that the atomic bomb had been successfully tested. (Churchill had long been aware of the Manhattan Project.) When Truman added that FDR had left instructions that he was to inform Stalin, too, Churchill implored him not to. But Truman insisted. Churchill then said, "If you have to tell him, Mr. President, include it in a whole raft of new military developments—a new tank, a new airplane, the situation in the Kurile Islands—and then slip in 'a new bomb' in the middle."

Truman did just that. Although it is possible that Stalin knew of the bomb through his spies, when it was dropped a month later in Hiroshima, the infuriated Soviet premier summoned U.S. Ambassador Averell Harriman to the Kremlin. Harriman then coolly pointed to the notes at Potsdam.

Between a neophyte American president and an implacable Russian premier, Churchill was on edge. His mind was also distracted by the impending election news from London.

Postwar Campaign
In the 1945 Parliamentary elections, the Conservatives ran on Churchill's wartime record, reminding voters that Japan had not yet been beaten. But Labourites won by stressing the home front, with slogans like "Industry must *serve* the people—not enslave them!"

One morning Churchill awoke from a nightmare. He told an aide: "There in my dream I was on a hospital gurney and white-coated attendants pulled the sheet over my head. I was a corpse and I knew it was an omen of my defeat." To Churchill, the actual impact of the losing returns a couple of days later struck like "a savage blow."

Americans, many of whom did not understand the British parliamentary system, were incredulous. But Churchill, whose personal approval ratings were over 90 percent, was not a president running for reelection. He was just one of over 600 candidates of parliament facing election—and he easily won his own seat in Woodford. But the massive majority of those elected were Labourites, not Conservatives, thus mandating a Labour prime minister—Clement Attlee.

Still, Churchill was stunned that the British people, whom he had so recently led to triumphant victory, would, by turning out the Conservative Party, send him out of office. The bannered postmortems of the British press didn't help. First, they said it was his very fame as a world statesman that had toppled him from office. Somehow, the British people felt that Churchill, the war leader, would not be as dedicated to the homely problems of a job for the returning veteran, a better pension for Dad, or relief for Mum's mounting medical bills. Then, in an even more ironic twist, some newspaper pundits assigned the blame for the Conservative defeat on, of all things, Churchill's speeches—claiming his partisan diatribes against the "monster" of socialism diminished his credibility. Swing voters, as well as socialists, were apparently infuriated by Churchill's eve-of-the-election charge:

"I declare to you, from the bottom of my heart, that the socialist system cannot be established without a political police . . . they would have to fall back on some kind of Gestapo, no doubt very humanely directed in the first instance."

His former socialist allies in the coalition government were stung by the ill-considered comparison to Hitler's henchmen. Churchill had wounded himself more than his Labourite opponents, said the newspapers. A national hero had abased himself through political cant, they charged. From political hack, the commentators wrote, it was but a short step to political has-been.

For Churchill, leaving 10 Downing Street was a shock. Not since Gallipoli had he sustained such a crippling blow. Clementine, thinking of his advancing age and his health, tried to console him. "Winston," she said, "it may well be a blessing in disguise."

"At the moment," replied Churchill, "it seems quite effectively disguised."

SARAH CHURCHILL

Churchill saw reflected in daughter Sarah his own irrepressible creativity and stubborn independence. Indeed, Sarah became his most famous offspring—and in one of the few fields he left alone: showbiz. Sarah was born in 1914 and took up ballet as a child. By the age of 17 she was dancing professionally. In 1936 she made her professional theatrical debut in *Follow the Sun* on the London stage. (She was a chorus girl.) By 1940 she was appearing in British stage and film dramas, but when war broke out she enlisted in the WAAF, the British equivalent of the Women's Army Corps.

Sarah Churchill (with Fred Astaire in a scene from *Royal Wedding*) was nicknamed "Mule" by her father. Her three marriages and problems with alcohol caused her parents much concern.

In 1949 she first toured America in *Philadelphia Story*, making her Broadway debut two years later in *Gramercy Ghost*. She came to Hollywood at the suggestion of her friend Peter Lawford, but made only a few films. The most notable was 1951's *Royal Wedding*, in which she co-starred with Fred Astaire.

Like her father, Sarah also painted, and she wrote books of poetry. She died in 1982.

King George wanted to appoint him a peer of the realm—the Duke of London—but Churchill would not consider retiring from the House of Commons. His Majesty then suggested conferring upon Churchill the palace's highest honor, the Knight of the Garter. Churchill replied: "I could not accept the Order of the Garter from my Sovereign when I had received the 'Order of the Boot' from his people." (He would later accept it in 1953 at the coronation of George's daughter Elizabeth.)

The kings and queens of Norway, Denmark, and Holland, who had invited him to their courts, were also spurned. Conservative Party leaders tried to map a global tour of the British Empire, as well as Europe, for him. More than a few cities in Canada and Australia, as well as in Britain, were ready to offer him their ceremonial gold keys, with the accompanying appropriate civic celebrations to honor the war's most heroic figure. Churchill saw these tributes, though, as another not-so-subtle hint that he resign his leadership of the Conservative Party. "I refuse," said Churchill, "to be exhibited like a prize bull at a county fair whose chief attraction is his past prowess."

> "Of all the talents bestowed upon men, none is so precious as the gift of oratory. He who enjoys it wields a power more durable than that of a great king."
>
> WINSTON CHURCHILL

Clement Attlee, the Labour Party leader, had now moved into 10 Downing Street. Churchill's home at Chartwell had become expensive to maintain, and he decided to put it up for sale. (In 1946 a group of investors bought the house for the National Trust, allowing Churchill to spend the rest of his life there for a "rent" of just £350 a year.)

In London he and Clementine moved into Claridge's, the premier hotel. The chairman of the Savoy group of hotels, Hugh Watner, gave him his own suite. Churchill, however, was uneasy with the balcony, which had an eighty-foot drop. After a few days, he told Watner: "I don't like sleeping near a precipice. I've no desire to quit the world, but desperate thoughts come into the head."

Churchill's old mental nemesis, the "black dog," filled his hours. To recuperate, he flew to Italy, where Field Marshal Alexander had given him his villa on Lake Como, which his armies had commandeered. After a week of no mail or newspapers, the glazed numbness in Churchill began to thaw. Three decades earlier, he had taken up painting to get his mind off the

Gallipoli disaster. Now, armed with brush and oils, Churchill turned to painting again, and he eyed the lake and hills as subjects for his canvas.

Painting was more than a pastime for Churchill; it became his lifeline. The oils on his palette were medicines for his mind, and the brushes swept away blackness of his mood. There under the sunny Italian skies and the blue Lake Como that shimmered underneath, Churchill applied his own therapy of landscape painting. He called them "seascapes," and they were to him tonics of "bottled sunshine."

While at Lake Como, another sort of medicine reached in the form of a letter—on White House stationery. It was an invitation to speak at a small college in Fulton, Missouri, with a name that amused Churchill: Westminster College. Major General Harry Vaughan, Truman's military aide and an alumnus of the college, had conceived the idea of inviting Churchill. Vaughan asked Truman if he would pen a note to the bottom of the invitation letter by the college president, to ensure an immediate response from Churchill. So Truman wrote: "It's a fine college in my state. Come and I'll introduce you." Thus Truman was guaranteeing his own appearance at Westminster if Churchill accepted.

To be introduced for an address by the president of the United States—even if at a small college in a small town he had never heard of—would be an international headline for the ex–prime minister. Churchill, as head of the defeated party, may have had no real political power, but he had now been handed a podium with a world audience. The voice that had commanded armies around the globe could still move the forces of international opinion.

When Churchill returned from Italy, the Conservatives had reassessed their earlier view that Churchill should step down as leader of the party. Polls showed that Churchill, far from being a liability, was an asset to the party, perhaps its only asset. Grumblings from the rank-and-file Conservatives abated as a more sober analysis of the Conservative defeat shifted the blame from the wartime premier to the party that had only reluctantly chosen him under the constraint of a national crisis.

The British electorate had not so much defeated Churchill as they had defeated the many Conservative Party members who had held office in the inglorious two decades before the war. Though Churchill was nominally a Conservative in that feckless time, he was also the Conservative government's most prominent opponent.

Unhappy Cold Warriors
Secretary of State James Byrnes (left, with President Truman) was trying to repair postwar differences with the Soviet Union and opposed Churchill's anticommunist saber rattling. Like many in the administration, Byrnes was particularly displeased by the Iron Curtain address.

In 1945, the British people compared the two parties—one which had a plan for a postwar welfare state, and another with no real idea for social reform over the last twenty years. In the end, they chose the program of one over the personality of the other.

Churchill now went to work to build such a program, as well as rebuild the party. He appointed a task force to develop a domestic program under the leadership of R. A. "Rab" Butler and assigned Lord Woolton the task of revamping the party at the grass roots. For himself, he charted a personal program of writing a history of World War II and playing the role of world statesman.

In January 1946, Churchill sailed on the *Queen Elizabeth* to New York and then took a train to Miami for some sun and sand before journeying to Washington. There he holed up in a British Embassy bedroom, making revisions to his Fulton speech, which he had entitled "Sinews of Peace." The title was a play on Cicero's phrase "sinews of war." Churchill was striking his familiar theme that only preparedness could ensure peace: the Soviet political and military encroachments could be stopped only by a united West under the resolute leadership of the United States. He wanted to jerk America out of its cozy belief in the United Nations, which he now regarded as ineffectual, and reveal the imperialism behind the Kremlin's mask of democracy.

Since the governments in Washington and London were reluctant to topple the illusion of peace that existed between the wartime allies, Churchill saw it as his duty to do so. As an out-of-office world statesman, he could sound the alarm that Prime Minister Attlee and President Truman hesitated to utter.

From the Truman administration came Dean Acheson, one of the president's favorite diplomats, to see Churchill at the embassy. The undersecretary of state came to offer suggestions to the text. Acheson found Churchill in the second-story bedroom, garbed in his dragon dressing gown, swathed in cigar smoke, and sipping whisky and soda as he polished and repolished the lines he had dictated in London before he had left. "If genius is the infinite capacity for taking pains, Churchill is overqualified," Acheson said later. One of Acheson's suggestions was to eliminate the reference to World War II as "the unnecessary war." Quite wisely, Acheson thought that right-wing Republicans would seize on the phrase as support for their past opposition to Roosevelt and as justification for a return to isolationism. The revised sentence now read: "There never was a war in all history easier to prevent by timely action." Acheson also recommended that Churchill make a reference to the United Nations.

On March 4, an impatient President Truman waited for Churchill, who arrived late at Union Station for the trip to Missouri on the *Ferdinand Magellan,* the presidential train. Standing at the open rear end of the lounge car, with the press milling beneath them, Truman pointed out to Churchill the presidential seal that is always carried with a traveling chief executive and

Freedom Train

Churchill and Truman nod farewell to the press as their train leaves Union Station in Washington, D.C., for Missouri on March 4, 1946. The former prime minister was considerably more jovial than the sitting president, who faced strong opposition in his own party.

The Curtain Falls
Churchill's Iron Curtain speech was considered shocking because it condemned America and Britain's wartime ally so soon after victory. Yet in hindsight, his dark vision of Soviet hegemony proved acute.

proudly revealed that he had recently redesigned it. "Mr. Churchill, the head of the eagle used to be turned right to face the arrows, but I had it changed to turn the other way to face the olive branches."

Churchill, whose speech the next day would cast shadows on the roseate glow of the immediate postwar peace, could not quite give the new seal his full approval. He told the president, in front of the listening press on hand: "Why not put the eagle's neck on a swivel so it could turn to the olive branch or the arrows as the occasion demands?"

The reporters laughed. Truman, a bit miffed at Churchill's quip at his expense, replied, "Well, let's have some whisky."

"Capital idea," said Churchill, and they ducked into the lounge. There, tumblers with ice and a bottle of Jack Daniel's were presented.

A dismayed Churchill exclaimed: "This isn't whisky—it's bourbon!" Churchill and Truman's military aide, Harry Vaughan, then went out and pulled the emergency cord. The train came to an immediate halt just outside Washington at Silver Springs, Maryland, where a case of Johnnie Walker Black was brought to the rescue. As the B&O train rolled through the town of Frederick in the countryside of western Maryland, Churchill regaled Truman, as he once had Roosevelt, with the thirty-couplet rendition of the Civil War poem "Barbara Frietchie," about the Union patriot-heroine of Frederick. John Greenleaf Whittier's poem reads: "'Shoot, if you must, this old gray head / But spare your country's flag,' she said."

Then Churchill retired to his stateroom for a nap and more work on his speech. When he emerged to rejoin the president for dinner, he offered his frequent complaint on American cocktail habits at that time: "Why do you Americans stop your drinking at dinner?"

Truman replied with a reference to the aid to Britain that was now being debated in Congress: "The cost of supplying you with wine would mean a bigger loan."

Churchill retorted, "You Americans keep trying to twist the 'loan's' tale."

Truman had read Churchill's text and given his approval. Advance copies had already been distributed to the press, but Churchill was still searching for the imagery that would define the thrust of his speech. Before midnight, the train stopped for refueling in Illinois. Churchill opened his curtain and saw a sign that read "Springfield, Home of Lincoln." Whether or not it was the ghost of Lincoln who inspired him, his closing of the compartment window curtain suggested the metaphor for Soviet tyranny.

When the train arrived the next morning in Jefferson City, a limousine awaited the president and the former prime minister. The motorcade was delayed temporarily until a long Havana could be purchased at a Jefferson

City tobacco store for Churchill, who needed the prop for the open car ride into Fulton and the Westminster College campus.

In his introduction, Truman was brusque: "Mr. Churchill and I believe in freedom of speech. I understand Mr. Churchill might have something useful to say."

Churchill began on a light note. With his hands clasping the sides of his scarlet (and honorary) Oxford robes, he peered over his black spectacles and harrumphed in his habitual stuttering style:

"I am glad to come to Westminster College… the name Westminster is somehow familiar to me. I seem to have heard of it before. Indeed it was at Westminster that I received a very large part of my education… "

Then to stress that he was no longer expressing British official policy, he said, "Let me…make it clear that I have no official mission of any kind and that I speak only for myself." He continued by asserting that the paramount mission facing the world was the prevention of another global war. Raising his forefinger twice in emphasis, he pointed to two institutions that would play major roles in the maintenance of peace—a strengthened United Nations Organization and the continuing "special relationship between Britain and America."

Then, with the epic foreboding of a Milton, Churchill began his celebrated description:

"A shadow has fallen upon the scenes so lately lighted by the Allied victory. From Stettin in the Baltic, to Trieste in the Adriatic, an iron curtain has descended across the Continent."

Potsdam Meeting
Churchill (with Truman and Stalin at Potsdam in July 1945) respected the instincts and judgment of the new U.S. president, but he also found Truman woefully unprepared by Roosevelt for dealing with the Soviets.

WORDSMITH

Churchill (speaking in 1949) loved Saxon words like *pluck*, *yoke*, *task*, and *flinch*. "Short words are best," he said, "and old words, when short, are best of all."

John F. Kennedy said that Churchill "mobilized the English language and sent it into battle." He usually won. Among the most famous phrases that Churchill coined are "iron curtain" and "summit meeting." He changed aeroplane to airplane and hydraplane to seaplane. He also invented the phrase "business as usual," way back in 1914.

He borrowed from the poet John Donne ("Mollify it with thy tears of sweat of blood.") to craft his 1940 speech: "I have nothing to offer you but blood, toil, tears and sweat." It became the rallying cry of England during the war.

Like most good speakers, Churchill had an ear for ringing sounds—and the uglier the better. The consonants *q*, *sq*, and *sn* were among his favorites for conveying invective. Thus enemies were *squalid* or *sniveling*; their very existence made him *queasy*. When searching for a new synonym to describe traitors, he hit upon the surname of a notorious Norwegian Nazi collaborator: Vidkun Quisling. Thus was born Churchill's famous line: "These vile quislings in our midst."

At the mention of "iron curtain," Churchill's clenched fists shook in angered dismay. Then, one by one, with finger pointing in mute chorus, he recited the litany of occupied cities:

"Behind that line lie all the capitals of the ancient states of Central and Eastern Europe: Warsaw, Berlin, Prague, Vienna, Budapest, Belgrade, Bucharest, and Sofia, all of these famous cities and the populations around them lie in what I must call the Soviet sphere, and are all subject in one form or another, not only to Soviet influence but to a very high and, in many cases, increasing measure of control from Moscow."

The "iron curtain passage," which Churchill had added in the night, was not included in the advance texts. Thus, some of the leading papers, such as the *Washington Post,* failed to mention the phrase in their coverage of the speech. Even the newsreels missed capturing it because the cameramen chose to wind their cameras at that point of the speech. (Indeed, there was almost no recording of the historic address, as the speaker system went dead for a minute. Fortunately, a former army signals operator, seated under the platform where attending veterans crouched because of the overflow audience, managed to fix it.)

The phrase, which made its public debut in this Fulton address, had in fact been used by Churchill before. In a telegram to Truman on May 6, 1945, he had written of his profound misgivings over the withdrawal of the American army to the occupation line: ". . . this bringing Soviet power into the heart of Western Europe and the descent of an iron curtain between us and everything to the eastward." Indeed, at Potsdam, Germany, Churchill had confronted Stalin with the phrase "iron fence." Stalin's reply was: "All fairy tales!"

Now though, "iron curtain" became part of the English language. Churchill then followed with an insight into the Kremlin mind that would never be surpassed in succeeding years:

"I do not believe that Soviet Russia desires war. What they desire is the fruits of war and the indefinite expansion of powers and doctrines."

For such Soviet imperialism, he offered this prescription:

"From what I have seen of our Russian friends and allies during the war, I am convinced there is nothing they admire so much as strength, and there is nothing for which they have less respect than weakness, especially military weakness."

Then he reinforced his postwar summons to action with a reminder of his prewar warning:

Cold War Tension
The uneasy alliance between Britain and the Soviet Union during World War II (as caricatured in this anti-Semitic propaganda poster) was shattered after Stalin installed puppet regimes in postwar Eastern Europe.

Divided Loyalties

Traveling to New York in March 1949 to support the forerunner of the North Atlantic Treaty Organization, Churchill was met by protesters who opposed such a pact as an affront to relations with the Soviet Union.

"Last time I saw it all coming and cried aloud to my fellow-countrymen and to the world, but no one paid any attention. Up to the year 1933 or even 1935, Germany might have been saved from the awful fate which has overtaken her and we might have all been spared the miseries Hitler let loose upon mankind. There never was a war in all history easier to prevent by timely action than the one which has just desolated such great areas of the globe. It could have been prevented in my belief without the firing of a single shot, and Germany might be powerful, prosperous, and honoured today; but no one would listen, and one by one we were all sucked into the awful whirlpool."

Newsreel cameras recorded the applauding of President Truman at the speech's conclusion, but no vocal or written endorsement of Churchill's speech ever appeared. In fact, the president distanced himself from the message. Truman was a shrewd enough politician to sense the firestorm of protest that would be triggered by a speech that accused our recent wartime ally of threatening the postwar peace. Neither the left wing of his own party nor much of the press would be happy with this attack on "Uncle Joe."

He was right. To appease his party's New York and Los Angeles wings, Truman denied that he had previously read the address. Dean Acheson was scheduled to speak at a dinner in New York honoring Churchill the next week; Truman ordered Acheson not to attend. Truman also cabled

Stalin to come to America and give his side of the story. He even offered to send the battleship *Missouri* to bring him across the Atlantic. (Stalin scorned the invitation.)

At Hyde Park, Roosevelt's widow called Churchill a "warmonger." Three Democratic senators held a press conference on the Capitol steps and described his speech as "shocking."

While Churchill succeeded in arousing American public opinion on Stalinism, he was puzzled by the hostility to his address. The *Nation* said that Churchill had "added a sizable bit of poison to the deteriorating relations." The *Wall Street Journal* said: "The United States wants no such alliance [against Russia]." Nobel prize–winning author Pearl Buck said: "We are now nearer to war."

In London, Prime Minister Attlee also backed away from the talk. This was a speech "in a foreign country…by a private individual." But if the speech gave the jitters to the British Foreign Office, and the U.S. State Department, Churchill, in his new role as traveling world statesman, was as happy as a boy let out of school. Free from the constraints that the responsibility of high office imposed, Churchill could offer proposals without worry of diplomatic niceties.

Two months after Fulton, he was at the Hague. There he told the Dutch what he had also told the Belgians months previously: "I see no reason why . . . there should not ultimately arise the United States of Europe."

Then, in September 1946, he astounded a Swiss audience at Zurich University by voicing the unthinkable, hardly a year after Germany surrendered:

"I am now going to say something that will astonish you. The first step in the re-creation of the European family must be a partnership between France and Germany. In this way only can France recover the moral leadership of Europe. There can be no revival of Europe without a spiritually great France and a spiritually great Germany."

The idea of Germany playing a role in the future of Europe hardly a year after the nation's defeat startled Churchill's audience at a time when the

CLEMENT ATTLEE

"Of all the Labour colleagues in the wartime coalition," said Churchill, "I respected Attlee the most."

Churchill famously described postwar Labour Prime Minister Clement Attlee as "a sheep in sheep's clothing" and "a modest man with much to be modest about." The mild-mannered Attlee may have looked like a clerk, but he was far from mediocre, and Churchill knew it. Born in 1883 to a well-to-do family, Attlee attended the prestigious Haileybury School and studied law at Oxford. Bored with the trappings of wealth, he entered social work and later gave up his practice of law to devote himself to politics as a means to improve working conditions. During World War I he was injured at Gallipoli, the disastrous invasion of Turkey that Churchill helped orchestrate. After the war, Major Attlee was elected as a Labour M.P.

After defeating Churchill in the first postwar election, Attlee moved into 10 Downing Street in July of 1945. For six years he administered a socialist-style government that, among other things, nationalized the electric, gas, coal, rail, and steel industries. He died in 1967.

horrors of Buchenwald were only first being heard at the Nuremberg trials. Churchill once had said: "If I can not be the kettle-drum, I might try to be the conductor." Churchill now found that he could strike some strident chords in foreign policy that as prime minister he would have had to mute.

Furthermore, as the opposition leader, Churchill found an inviting target in the bureaucratic bumbledum of the Labour Party. In its statist blueprint to reach "the New Jerusalem," the Labour government had nationalized key industries and instituted a national health system. Churchill impishly called it "government of the duds, by the duds, and for the duds." Paraphrasing the verse of Sir Walter Scott, he predicted that the Labourites would vanish "unwept, unhonored, unsung and unhung."

One forum for Churchill's rapier wit was London's Other Club, which had been co-founded by Churchill and his friend Lord Birkenhead as a place where the bright and witty in both parties, as well as authors and actors, could talk politics without restraint. One of the features of the group, which met at a private room in the Savoy Hotel, was a "topic of the day." The question one day in 1946 was "Who was the Father of Socialism?" Churchill said: "The founder of Socialism was Christopher Columbus. When he started, he didn't know where he was going; when he arrived, he didn't know where he was; and he did it all on borrowed money."

Poor Attlee, who followed Churchill as prime minister, lacked his predecessor's wit and humor. In personality, speeches, and appearance, the new leader seemed like a black-and-white film after Technicolor. A stenographer at 10 Downing Street who continued to work though the change in leadership, said, "Mr. Attlee is a pleasant man—and I'm sure he's a Christian gentleman. But after Churchill, it's like drinking water every day instead of champagne."

One day, Churchill entered the House of Commons lavatory to find Attlee standing at the near end of the long urinal. Churchill walked past him, all the way to the far end. Said Attlee, "Winston, I know we're political opponents, but we don't have to carry our differences into the gentlemen's lavatory."

Churchill replied, "Clement, the trouble with you socialists is that whenever you see anything in robust and sturdy condition, you want the government to regulate it."

At the time, investment in British industries had declined

Stumping for Office
Campaigning in 1951, Churchill said, "I am told of the popular slogan 'Labour gets things done,' but surely it should run, 'Labour gets things done in.' " The Conservatives won by a narrow margin, and the king asked Churchill to form a new government.

and productivity had stagnated. Other European countries, such as France and Belgium, were recovering faster. To answer the socialists, who promoted equality as their goal, Churchill growled: "Equality yes, there is 'equality' in socialism—the equality of misery, but I much prefer capitalism's inequality of wealth."

The House of Commons was his stage, and Churchill was a consummate actor. With his puckish green eyes peering above eyeglasses far set down upon his nose, he could instantly set up a laugh. Neither a Ronald Reagan nor Jay Leno was better.

A Labourite, Denis Palings, whose surname is the word for the pointed picket iron fence around the House of Commons, once called Churchill a "dirty dog capitalist" during debate.

Churchill replied, "My reaction to the gentleman's charge is that of any 'dirty dog' toward any 'palings.' "

Once in a debate, Hugh Gaitskell, the Labourite minister of fuel, suggested a regimen of fewer baths as a way to conserve coal: "Actually," said Gaitskell, "I never was fond of taking too many baths myself."

Victory Again

Churchill flashes a victory sign from the Conservative Party offices in Woodford after becoming prime minister for the second time, a month before his 77th birthday. Clementine (at the window) worried about his health.

Churchill interrupted: "Need we wonder why the prime minister and his cabinet are increasingly in bad odor?" And he added: "Could we admit, Mr. Speaker, the word 'lousy' as an expression referring to this administration, not in a contemptuous sense but purely as factual description?"

By the end of 1949, the Labourites were starting to smell in the polls, as the Conservatives began picking up seats in by-elections. Churchill was feisty at the thought of returning to power. On November 30, the morning of his seventy-fifth birthday, the press waited for him outside his London home at 28 Hyde Park Gate. A photographer said, "I hope, sir, that I will shoot your picture on your one-hundredth birthday."

Churchill surveyed the cameraman carefully and replied, "I don't see why not, young man. You look reasonably fit and healthy."

Full of vim and zest, Churchill wielded his wit like a lance to puncture the bureaucratic jargon of the Socialists. An opponent of "political correctness" decades before the term had been coined, Churchill poked fun at the Orwellian "newspeak" of left-wing academics and bureaucratic mandarins:

"I hope you have all mastered the official socialist jargon which our masters, as they call themselves, wish us to learn. You must not use the word 'poor.' They are described as 'the lower income group.' Then there is a lovely one about

Trigger Finger?
During the 1951 election, London's *Daily Mirror* portrayed Churchill as a warmonger, implying (in a series of illustrations) that as prime minister he would lead the world into nuclear holocaust. The charge stung Churchill, who had guided his country back to peace, and the paper apologized.

houses and homes. They are in the future to be called 'accommodation units.' I don't see how we are to sing our old song 'Home, Sweet Home.' I suppose we now must sing 'Accommodation Unit, Sweet Accommodation Unit.' I hope to live to see the British democracy spit all this rubbish from their lips."

On election day, the British people did unseat scores of Labourite members who had come to office in the landslide of 1945. But though the sizable gains by Conservatives shattered the overwhelming Labourite majority, it was not quite enough to return them to power. Though more Britons voted Conservative than Labour, they did not win more seats.

The slim margin of Labour's victory meant that another general election was in the offing. Churchill's eagerness to return to 10 Downing Street was no longer fired by a zeal to avenge his loss of 1945. It was lit by a new dream to find an accommodation between East and West that would lift the threat of nuclear war. The leader who had climaxed his long career by waging war wanted to close it by making peace.

Churchill first unveiled his hope of arranging a conference with the Soviets at a speech in Edinburgh in early 1950:

"Still I cannot help coming back to this idea of another talk with Soviet Russia upon the highest level. The idea appeals to me of a supreme effort to bridge a gulf between the two worlds, so that each can live their life, if not in friendship, at least without the hatreds of the cold war…It is not easy to see how things could be worsened by a parley at the summit."

But if his call for a summit meeting with Stalin found much acceptance in Britain, reaction in America was cool. Times had changed since the iron-curtain speech. The invasion of South Korea by Communist troops from the north and the conviction of Alger Hiss for lying about being a Soviet agent had rattled American nerves. In the United States, Stalin was now perceived to be as tyrannical as Hitler—except that the spread of communism was not confined to Europe.

The mood in Britain was different. Some of the left actually sided with North Korea against America, including the so-called "Red Dean" of Canterbury, Dr. Hewlett Johnson, and Lord Jowitt, the Labour lord chancellor. When some Labour members of Parliament attacked America's role in Korea, Churchill rebuked them for disloyalty to British troops who were fighting alongside their American allies.

President Truman, who had initiated the "police action" in Korea, was now spearheading the West's defenses against the advance of Communism, including the Marshall Plan to aid Europe and the founding of NATO (the North Atlantic Treaty Organization). Opposition leader Churchill saluted Truman's leadership.

Now that President Truman was turning the eagle's head toward the arrows, Churchill was taking another look at the olive branch. He was convinced that there must be some way for the democratic nations of the West to coexist with the Communist bloc.

In the general election of 1951, the old warrior made peace his campaign theme. But his opponents denounced him as a warmonger. The socialists countered with a caricature in the *Daily Mirror,* their newspaper house organ, that showed Churchill next to a bomb and asking the question: "Whose finger do you want on the nuclear trigger?"

Churchill answered: "I do not hold that we should rearm to fight. I hold that we should rearm to parley."

Labour replied: "It's not that Churchill wants war, but that he doesn't know how to avoid it."

On the eve of the election, Churchill journeyed to Plymouth to campaign for his son Randolph, who was standing for election there. Churchill said that he himself remained in public life only because he thought he could still make a lasting contribution to peace. "I pray indeed," he allowed, "that I may have this opportunity. It is the last prize I seek."

On election day, Churchill got that opportunity. The Conservatives eked out a victory, and Churchill was back at 10 Downing Street.

Uphill Work

"I do hope Winston will be able to help the country," Clementine (with Winston the night before the election) wrote in a letter to a friend. "It will be up-hill work, but he has a willing, eager heart."

Prime Minister Again
1951–1955

I t is currently fashionable for academics to downplay the second Churchill ministry—as it is to diminish the Eisenhower presidency of roughly the same period—as less than distinguished. Yet both tenures, if anticlimactic in the careers of both men, were times of sunny stability and fruitful consolidation on the domestic front. Indeed, historians such as A. L. Rowse and Alan Moorehead credit Churchill with presiding over one of the most felicitous administrations in British history.

For starters, Churchill waged war against "Queutopia," his phrase describing the long lines for consumer goods and services in a tightly regulated society. (His efforts were only partly successful in a country where politely standing in line for buses is part of the national identity.) He denationalized the iron and steel industries, and most rationing was lifted. He assembled a cabinet of future prime ministers such as Anthony Eden, Harold Macmillan, and Alec Douglas-Home.

Still, the seventy-seven-year-old prime minister tended to delegate the agenda for domestic programs; foreign affairs were his focus. His quest was, in his words, "world easement." "We arm to parley" was his maxim. In his eye, the strengthening of Western defenses was not only a necessity for security but a key to future negotiations. He knew that arms buildup was costly for the Soviets; any settlement to defuse the Cold War tensions would have to be predicated on Soviet self-interest.

THE CHECKERS SPEECH

On September 24, 1952, vice-presidential nominee Richard Nixon went on television to deny that he misused political contributions and gifts. In the speech, Nixon famously said, "I am not a quitter," described his wife Pat's coat as "a respectable Republican cloth coat," and said he would not return a cocker spaniel puppy given to his daughter Tricia, who, he said, had named the pooch Checkers.

Lion Tamer

In 1943, Churchill's "pet" lion Rota (snacking at London's Zoological Gardens on July 26, 1942) sired four cubs, which were named Alamein, Bizerte, Mareth, and Tunis—after North African cities where the Germans were routed during the war.

One of his first trips as prime minister outside London was to France, to visit his old friend General Eisenhower. President Truman had appointed Eisenhower to head the newly formed NATO command.

He found the usually sunny Ike testy. At a December luncheon at Marnes-la-Coquette, Eisenhower's villa west of Paris, the general complained throughout lunch about the failure of the Western European nations—including Britain—to commit the necessary troops to NATO. He dwelled on this theme well into the dessert course. Finally, a thirsty Churchill, who had been eyeing an ornate credenza behind Eisenhower on which a decanter of brandy stood, said, "Ike, that's a handsome credenza. Is it *Louis Seize*?"

Eisenhower—despite a nudge by his deputy, General Alfred Gruenther—said: "I guess it is. It was here when I came," and went on speaking about the need to enlarge the British contingent.

Then Churchill interjected: "And that's a splendid decanter on the credenza. Is it Austrian crystal?"

Ike replied, "I suppose, but about this manpower problem—"

Whereupon Churchill again interrupted: "More than manpower, it's morale—and the first thing the supreme Allied commander must do is lift the 'spirits' on that credenza." In his toast to Ike, he said that only General Eisenhower could "lift the spirits of Europe" by visiting the Continent's parliaments. Yet Churchill's paramount goal was a summit conference with Stalin that might thaw the freeze of the Cold War.

Like Eisenhower, who had recently bought a farm in Gettysburg, Pennsylvania, Churchill relished life as a country squire. To spend more time at Chartwell, he lengthened his weekends to four days, leaving Deputy Prime Minister and Foreign Secretary Anthony Eden to stand in for him at the House of Commons on Mondays.

At Chartwell, he was a figure in the community. He showed up to exhibit his cattle—shorthorn beef and Jersey dairy cows—in the agriculture fair. Churchill was only sorry that the law would not allow his pet lion, Rota, housed in the London Zoo, to live at Chartwell. During the wartime meat shortage, Churchill once had threatened a sloppy clerk: "If you fail for a third time, you will be Rota's din-din!" The clerk quit in terror.

He sometimes rode, even in his late seventies, in county hunts. But Churchill seldom attended his parish church, at St. Margaret's, in Westerham. When he appeared one Easter morning, the rector said: "You can't say, Prime Minister, that you are a pillar of the church." "No," replied Churchill. "I'm a flying buttress. I support it from the outside."

In his second tenure as prime minister, Churchill weekended less frequently at Chequers because his attachments to Chartwell had grown too strong. Also, the staff at the official prime minister's residence in Buckinghamshire was not as indulgent with his mischievous grandchildren. But Churchill was at Chequers in February 1952, when he heard that the ailing King George VI had died. Britain had a new monarch—a twenty-five-year-old woman. Her coronation was the Indian summer of Churchill's life.

He was not alone. All Britain seemed to brighten with the dream of a new Elizabethan Age. The doldrums of the immediate postwar years had depressed the English people. Devaluation of the pound had left the victors of the war with one of the lowest living standards in Western Europe. Scarcity of goods and fuel shortages were commonplace. But the emergence of a young monarch, coinciding with the return of Churchill as prime minister, revived hopes for new glory.

Thus 1953 arrived with the splendid spectacle of a coronation year, as well as the inauguration of Winston's old friend Eisenhower as U.S. president. Yet at 10 Downing Street, Churchill greeted the American election with ambivalence. On the one hand, he was delighted that his old friend was president. Yet he worried that the Republican Party, after twenty years out of office, would not be amenable, but angry. Some of the isolationist views of Senator Robert Taft and other Republicans who now controlled Congress disturbed him.

Then came the reckless charges of Senator Joseph McCarthy, which Churchill felt undermined genuine anticommunist endeavors. Yet Churchill worried that the ugliness in the recent presidential campaign—in which Republican politicians attacked Roosevelt's "sellout" at Yalta—would compromise any meeting between Eisenhower and the Soviets.

Churchill left for the United States on New Year's Eve 1952. Most of the time he worked with his parliamentary secretary, John Colville, on their agenda with President-elect Eisenhower. The preparation mainly involved questions about dealing with the Soviet Union. Colville asked Churchill: "Prime Minister, when do you think the Cold War will end and the 'Iron Curtain' come down?"

Storybook Queen

"All the film people in the world, if they had scoured the globe, could not have found anyone so suited to the part," said Churchill of Queen Elizabeth (at her coronation in 1953).

ANIMAL MAGNETISM

Churchill loved pets and, as usual, he had his own distinct view on the subject: "Dogs look up to you, cats look down on you," he said. "Give me a pig—he just looks you in the eye and treats you as an equal." Churchill, in fact, kept a Chartwell menagerie that included pigs, lambs, and birds, as well as cats and dogs. Two pet swans patrolled his pond.

His favorite dog was Rufus, a poodle. Once Rufus wandered into a cabinet meeting at 10 Downing Street. At the empty chair next to his master, Rufus stood up on his legs in expectant attention. "No, Rufus," the prime minister said. "I haven't yet found it necessary to ask you to join the wartime cabinet."

Churchill also nurtured a black cat named Nelson, after the legendary British admiral. During a nighttime

Churchill named his dog Rufus (seen here in 1950) after William Rufus, the redheaded son and successor of William the Conqueror. After Rufus was killed in an accident in 1952, another Rufus took his place.

air raid, Nelson cowered under the bed in Churchill's underground War Rooms. "Nelson," Churchill roared, quoting the words of Shakespeare in *Henry V,* "summon the spirit of the tiger." Nelson made no move. "Think of your namesake. No one named Nelson slinks under a bed in time of crisis." Nelson, who was no scaredy-cat, reappeared.

Amazingly, one of Churchill's pets was still alive in 2002. His macaw parrot, Charlie, believed to be at least 103 years old, now lives at a garden center in Surrey. Charlie still curses a blue streak, thanks to the choice words Churchill taught him during World War II.

"How old are you, Jock?" Churchill asked.

"Thirty-seven," Colville answered.

"If you live to be seventy-five or about my age, you should see it happen." Churchill reasoned that the Soviet victory against Germany reinforced the legitimacy of the Communist regime, and that it would take two more generations before Eastern Europeans recognized the false promise of Marxism. (Colville died in November 1989 at age seventy-one, the very month that the Berlin Wall came down.)

On landing in New York, Churchill and Clementine met Eisenhower at Bernard Baruch's apartment on the Upper East Side. It was fitting that they talked about the Cold War in the home of their friend Baruch, who had coined the term in 1948. Churchill and Eisenhower agreed that the Cold War had to be waged as a war of ideas. Said Churchill: "It is not only important to discover truth, but also to know how to present it." Truth, Churchill argued, was the supreme weapon in the arsenal of the Free World, and it should be wielded, he said, like a searchlight into the crannies and corners of communism.

Three days later, Eisenhower, along with Secretary of State-designate John Foster Dulles, met Churchill again at Eisenhower's campaign office at New York's Commodore Hotel. On one vital matter, Churchill gave his reluctant consent for Eisenhower to threaten the use of the atom bomb to force a settlement of the Korean War. Armed with that threat, Eisenhower ended the conflict in June. (At the same time in Asia, British forces defeated Communist guerrillas in Malaysia.) Churchill then raised the idea of a summit conference with Stalin, but Dulles vehemently opposed it.

Churchill was back at 10 Downing Street on March 5, 1953, when the news flashed about Stalin's death. It was the seventh anniversary of his Iron Curtain address in Fulton, Missouri. Was there a chance now that the curtain might be parted a bit? He telegraphed Eisenhower for his reaction to a summit meeting with the new leader, Georgi Malenkov. Eisenhower was negative, but Churchill hoped to convince him.

At home, brighter events lightened Churchill's mind. For Coronation Day in 1953, the young queen made Churchill a Knight of the Garter—not coincidentally, on the day of England's patron saint,

Power Brokers
In New York to meet with the president-elect Eisenhower in January 1953, Churchill stopped by the apartment of his old friend Bernard Baruch to visit with (from left) Secretary of State designate John Foster Dulles, Baruch, and ambassador designate to Britain Winthrop Aldrich.

JOHN FOSTER DULLES

During a 1953 luncheon at 10 Downing Street, Secretary of State John Foster Dulles (left) opposed a summit meeting with the Soviets.

Churchill often crossed swords with John Foster Dulles, President Eisenhower's secretary of state—once describing the dour Calvinist lawyer as "Dull, Duller, Dulles." A prominent layman in the Presbyterian Church, Dulles came from a line of worldy bluebloods: His grandfather had been secretary of state under Benjamin Harrison, and his uncle held the same job under Woodrow Wilson.

Dulles himself resented the intimate relationship between Ike and Winston. And he was particularly hostile to the British prime minister's call for a summit meeting with the Soviets. When Dulles called for a Cold War strategy of "massive retaliation," Churchill said, "He is the only bull I know who carries his own china shop around with him."

Yet Churchill paid his respects to a dying Dulles in 1959. The former prime minister had been visiting President Eisenhower as a private citizen; before flying back to Britain, he stopped by Walter Reed Hospital to say good-bye to his old adversary.

George, who, like Churchill, had slain a dragon in defense of his country. He was now the second Sir Winston Churchill, the first having been his 17th-century ancestor who served in Parliament, attended the court of King Charles II, and fathered John, Duke of Marlborough.

The circle was closing for the seventy-eight-year-old parliamentarian who had begun his career in the reign of the last queen. On Coronation Day, June 2, with skies mixing sun and rain, the new Sir Winston was the only one to ride from Buckingham Palace in an open carriage past the joyously waving crowds that lined the procession route to Westminster.

The celebration following the coronation had hardly passed before Churchill was felled by a severe stroke. He had been overburdened with duties. The departure of Anthony Eden to Boston for a serious intestinal operation had made Churchill's responsibilities heavier. In addition, the banquets, receptions, and public appearances during the Coronation had added to the strain. Even a younger man would have been taxed to the limit.

At a June 26 dinner at 10 Downing Street for Premier De Gasperi of Italy, Churchill suddenly slumped over in his seat. The next day an announcement said that Sir Winston, on the advice of the doctors, was to rest for a month. What the country did not know was that Lord Moran, his doctor, feared he would die within days. Churchill was taken to Chartwell to recover. Some thought the paralyzed Churchill would never talk, much less walk, again.

But the old warrior rallied. Nursed by Clementine, Churchill was walking by July, seeing his key ministers and signing state papers. At the end of the summer, he went to the races as the guest of the queen, who then invited him to vacation with her at Balmoral, her Scottish castle.

In October Churchill won the Nobel Prize for Literature, which would be awarded in Stockholm in December. The citation described him as a "Caesar who wielded Cicero's pen." The announcement of the prize also encouraged speculation that he would retire at the Conservative Party conference, but he stunned the delegates with an hourlong address, concluding:

"If I stay, for the time being, bearing the burden at my age, it is not because of love for power or office. I have had an ample share of both. If I stay, it is because I have the feeling that I may, through things that have happened, have an influence on what I care about above all else—the heralding of a sure and lasting peace."

At the end of his speech, the convention of Conservative dignitaries and party officials rose to their feet and roared their salute to this tour de force of stamina. For Churchill, it was a sovereign display of willpower over physical frailty.

Churchill won the Nobel prize for literature, but he had wanted to win it for peace. To that end, he traveled to Bermuda in November for a meeting with Eisenhower and Prime Minister Joseph Laniel of France. Unfortunately, he failed to convince Ike of the wisdom of a conference with Russian Premier Malenkov. Eisenhower's doubts were fortified by Secretary of State Dulles. The sticking point was Malenkov's insistence that the People's Republic of China be included.

At the Bermuda meeting, Churchill and Eisenhower joined their efforts to convince the French to enter the European Defense Community—and to consider the inclusion of a small German contingent. But Churchill was annoyed by Dulles, who hovered over Eisenhower and bandied threats of nuclear force. Still, Churchill believed atomic testing was necessary, and that

Knight to Remember
The newly knighted Sir Winston Churchill rides with Clementine (now Lady Churchill) to the coronation of Elizabeth at Westminster Abbey in June 1953. Elizabeth is one of just four monarchs in British history to have reigned a half century or more. (The record of 63 years is held by her great-great-grandmother Victoria.)

possession of the bomb would prevent World War III. "Both sides know that it would begin with horrors of a kind and on a scale never dreamt before by human beings," he said.

By the summer of 1954, Churchill's stamina was clearly ebbing. Just about all of his Cabinet members were nudging, if not pushing, him out the door of 10 Downing Street. In June he decided to make one last bid for a summit, arriving in Washington on June 25. He was met at the airport by Vice President Nixon; together in an open motorcade, they rode to the White House. Nixon said later of their meeting:

"I had been told that he was not half the man he used to be, and at the luncheon it did seem he was dozing or at least inattentive as others spoke. But when he arose to address the audience, he wove the remarks of others at the head table masterfully into a powerful address. He talked about 'trade, not aid,' and argued for a strong deterrent defense. ('Peace is our aim and strength is the only way to get it.') All was laced with wit, anecdotes, and allusions to history.

"Afterwards I spent some time with him. If he was, indeed, 'half the man he used to be,' he was the most brilliant, insightful and commanding presence I have ever known."

THE LION AND THE MASTERPIECE

Don't try this at home: Churchill "improved" Peter Paul Rubens' *Lion and the Mouse.*

Chequers, the weekend retreat of Britain's prime ministers, is filled with magnificent paintings—none more famous than Rubens's *The Lion and the Mouse.* The painting depicts the moment in the classic Aesop fable when the mouse gnaws at the rope that binds the lion. Churchill, who thought the mouse was too small to accomplish that task, retouched the Baroque masterpiece to make the mouse larger. Despite his defacing, the value of the painting has increased.

At the White House, Eisenhower finally agreed to Churchill's request for a high-level meeting with the Soviets in a neutral city. Churchill asked if he might go to Moscow first to see if such a summit meeting was worthwhile, and Ike gave his approval. It was Eisenhower's position that the growing deterrent of NATO put the West into a position of strength in dealing with the Soviets. Their joint communiqué on June 29 stated: "The German Federal Republic should now take its place as an equal partner in the community of Western nations where it can make its proper contribution to the defense of the free world."

To sell his idea for a summit, Churchill talked to a group of congressmen at a luncheon. "Meeting jaw to jaw is better than war," he said waving his cigar in emphasis.

On the matter of war, Churchill advised Eisenhower not to commit any troops or equipment to the French, who were battling Ho Chi Minh in Indochina. This counsel fell on willing ears. Now that the war was ended in Korea, Eisenhower was not about to involve himself in another Asian conflict by assisting the French in their stand at Dien Bien Phu.

Although Churchill was attacked for not favoring extension of military aid to the French in Vietnam, it was a decision in hindsight that grows increasingly prescient in the light of the bloody cost that would be paid in the next decade.

Another sensitive matter that Churchill and Eisenhower discussed was atomic energy. In Bermuda, they talked of forming of an international atomic agency. Eisenhower fleshed out these ideas for Churchill's comment and reactions.

One phrase Churchill had changed was the earlier language that the "United States was free to use the atom bomb" to "[was] reserving the right to use the atomic bomb."

In December 1954, Eisenhower would propose his historic "Atoms for Peace" plan to the United Nations, which emanated from the White House meeting with Churchill. It was universally applauded by all nations, except those in the Soviet bloc.

On his return in July 1954 to 10 Downing Street, Churchill's cabinet treated his summit proposal with scorn. Still, Churchill resisted pleas from Eden, now also his nephew-in-law, to resign. (Eden had married Clarissa Churchill, daughter of Winston's brother Jack, in 1953.)

Most of Britain believed Churchill would resign on his eightieth birthday—November 30, 1954. The birthday occasion would be an unprecedented celebration in the House of Commons, equaled only by that

DAILY EXPRESS   **NOV. 12, 1954**

CROWDS BOO RUSSIAN AT HIGHBURY

ROW OVER RUSSIAN REFEREE

"Now that tension is lessened, perhaps we might have a top-level meeting to call off sporting events..."
London Express Service

Soccer Summit?

A 1954 cartoon poked fun at hopes that the death of Stalin would ease Cold War tensions. The cartoon depicts Churchill phoning new Soviet premier Georgi Malenkov to defuse a flap over a Russian soccer referee. Note the doves of peace perched on each leader's shoulder; the Russian dove is a wind-up toy.

> "Let there be sunshine on both sides of the Iron Curtain; and if ever the sunshine be equal on both sides, the Curtain will be no more."

WINSTON CHURCHILL

for Victoria's Jubilee. In Westminster Hall, around which the whirl of ten centuries of history had revolved, people of all parties assembled to pay tribute to the man who was the living embodiment of Parliament. The V sign was tapped out in Morse code on a drum as Sir Winston entered the Commons. After many speeches, the House presented him with a portrait painted by Graham Sutherland.

Churchill, who detested the painting, was droll and discreet in his comment: "It looks like a remarkable example of modern art." (Clementine later destroyed it.)

THE WEEKLY NEWSMAGAZINE

PRIME MINISTER CHURCHILL
Another opportunity for greatness.

In the Spotlight
The November 4, 1951, cover of
Time heralded Churchill's return to
10 Downing Street as "Another
opportunity for greatness." A year
earlier, the magazine had dubbed
him "Man of the Half Century."

But contrary to all the speculation, the old man did
not announce his retirement. Churchill, who felt his
influence and prestige were still needed, stayed on.
Indeed, perhaps only Churchill could have committed
Britain to the development of the hydrogen bomb.
The soldier who fought in Britain's last cavalry charge
in February 1898 would give the order to set off Britain's
first hydrogen bomb test in February 1955.

Despite his age, Churchill the parliamentarian could
still parry sharp jabs at Question Time with the droll
geniality of Dickens's Mr. Pickwick. One voluble member
who became enmeshed in the complexity of his own
question was advised: "Try one question at a time."
When another persistent member introduced a series of
questions with "Isn't it a fact…" Churchill brushed him
aside, saying: "The honourable gentleman seems more
desirous of imparting information than securing it."

But the old man's powers were flagging. He had
run his course, and he knew it. On the first of March,
Churchill delivered his last speech as prime minister,
in the debate introducing the annual White Paper on
national defense. Roy Jenkins, the future chancellor of the Exchequer and
later chancellor of Oxford, heard it as a Labourite M.P. He was moved by
Churchill's eloquence when he called for the United States and Britain to
devise "a balanced and phased system of disarmament," with verifiable
inspection controls. Until that was achieved, said Churchill, the only sane
policy for the Free World was defense by deterrence:

"Which way shall we turn to save our lives and the future of the world?
It does not matter to the old; they are going soon anyway. But I find it
repugnant to look at youth in all its activity and vigour and wonder what
would lie before them if God wearied of mankind."

Then he closed with words that might have made a fitting epitaph for
his life:

"The day may dawn when fair play, love for one's fellow men, respect for
justice and freedom, will enable tormented generations to march forth serene
and triumphant from the hideous epoch in which we have to dwell.
Meanwhile, never flinch, never weary, never despair."

It now remained for him to pass the leadership to Anthony Eden.
As Churchill joked to his cabinet: "I must retire. Anthony won't live
forever." On the night of April 4, the queen, in an unprecedented act,
came to dinner at 10 Downing Street to toast her departing prime
minister. She again offered him a dukedom, as her father once had,
which he declined.

The crowds that gathered outside the prime minister's official
residence that night saw the venerable prime minister assist the young

queen to her limousine. Then, with Churchill's deep bow of homage and Lady Churchill's graceful curtsy, the waving queen was driven off.

For a moment Sir Winston, in white tie and with the blue Knight of the Garter sash, stood framed against the doorway of 10 Downing Street. The onlookers were silent, as if reverently participating in an historic moment. Then they cheered.

The next day he went to Buckingham Palace to resign.

Royal Engagement

Queen Elizabeth leaves 10 Downing Street after her April 4, 1955, dinner with Winston and Clementine (in background). It was the first time that a British monarch dined at the prime minister's residence. Churchill, then 80, resigned the next morning.

World Symbol
1956–1965

The resignation of Churchill prompted a general election. A Conservative Party victory confirmed Anthony Eden as the new prime minister. If the vote was a referendum, the massive majority for the Conservatives was a testament to the British people's appreciation of Churchill's service.

Churchill now repaired to Chartwell. "To resign," he said, "was not to retire." For one thing, he wanted to finish his four-volume work, *The History of the English-Speaking Peoples,* whose writing had been interrupted by World War II.

Yet as he left the world stage, international affairs still commanded his attention. Only months after he left Downing Street, he followed with interest the first East-West summit meeting. In place of him at Geneva was his successor Eden who, along with Eisenhower, met the new Soviet premier, Nikolai Bulganin. (Malenkov had been forced out as the scapegoat for food shortages brought on by the government's failed agricultural policy.) The "Spirit of Geneva" was briefly hailed and saluted, but it disappeared as quickly as a week of sunshine in England. Churchill once gave his formula for a successful summit: "First policy, then place, and finally atmospherics."

A year later, in 1956, Eden stumbled at Suez. Churchill was astonished that Eden would attempt an Anglo-French-Israeli invasion of Egypt to safeguard the canal without informing President Eisenhower. From Eisenhower's point of view, it had been ill-timed, coming right before the vote for his reelection and, more importantly, just after Russia's invasion of Hungary to suppress an anti-communist rebellion.

Churchill was dismayed by this fracture of "the special relationship" between Britain and America. Though out of office, he wrote letters to Eisenhower on the importance of reestablishing a common front as soon as possible. When Jock Colville asked Churchill what he would have done in Eden's place, Churchill replied, "I would never have dared, and if I had dared, I would never have dared stop."

In January 1957, Eden, beset by illness and besieged by criticism of his actions at Suez, resigned. Again, the choice of Eden's successor was not clear. Rab Butler, the chancellor of the Exchequer, was a possibility. He was the deputy prime minister and seemed to many Conservative members of parliament a logical choice. Yet Butler was not as popular as Harold Macmillan with the rank-and-file party membership in the constituencies. The queen called Churchill to Buckingham Palace for advice. He promptly recommended Macmillan, who, unlike Butler, had sided with him in the 1930s in his attacks on the appeasement policies of the government. The queen chose Macmillan.

The following July, Churchill delivered his last major address. Speaking in front of the American Bar Association, which was meeting in London, Churchill warned about the direction the United Nations was taking. For one thing, he said, dictatorships were beginning to outnumber the democratic nations in the Assembly. The U.N., he charged, was becoming impotent:

"There are many cases where the United Nations have failed…Hungary is in my mind. Justice cannot be a hit-or-miss system. We cannot be content with an arrangement where our system of international laws apply only to those who are willing to keep them."

In May 1959, Churchill, still a member of Parliament, made a visit to Washington to see President Eisenhower. At Gettysburg, over whisky and water, the two statesmen ruminated how bigness in government, industry, corporations, universities, and the military in the new technological society might stifle the spark of the individual genius in a free society. Out of that discussion came some of the themes for Eisenhower's farewell address a year and a half later. "In the councils of government we must guard against the acquisition of unwarranted influence, sought or unsought, by the military industrial complex," he famously said, adding that U.S. defenses should be second to none.

On May 6, in rainy cold weather, Churchill spent his last day in the American capital. At Andrews Air Force Base, a crowd—mostly of reporters—gathered to see Churchill on what some thought might be his last visit to America. The old man shuffled his way slowly across the tarmac as the crowd clapped rhythmically. As Churchill mounted the steps to the

Macmillan Takes Charge
After the Suez debacle, Queen Elizabeth (at the urging of Churchill) called on Harold Macmillan (shown in 1957) to succeed Anthony Eden as prime minister. Macmillan said of Churchill, "Our finest hour and our greatest moment came from our work with him."

plane one at a time, the rain suddenly stopped in the late afternoon twilight. The horizon loomed pink.

Churchill, cigar in hand, turned and said, "Farewell to the land…[and then he paused]…of my mother." He waved his hand in a V sign. "God bless you all—good night!"

It was a time for farewells and the finishing of old business. In October 1959 at Woodford, Churchill stood for Parliament one last time. The crowd that gathered at the rally inside a school for his one campaign speech got a glimpse of a hunched-over, blanketed Churchill who was staring vacant-eyed from a platform chair. Yet once the old campaigner was introduced and helped to his feet, his sense of theater took over and the old impishness lit up his sagging features:

"Among our socialist friends there is great confusion about private enterprise," he said, assembling each word carefully into place. Then, raising his arms as if aiming a rifle, he continued: "Some see it as a predatory animal like a tiger to be shot. Others," he said, changing his hands to the pumping of a milker, "see it as a cow to be milked." As the crowd cheered his antics, he went on: "Only a handful see it for what it really is—the strong and willing horse that pulls the whole cart of the economy along." It was the final campaign speech of the old Tory, and it ended in laughter.

Churchill and the Conservatives won, but only rarely did Churchill now come to the Commons. When he did, it was an occasion. On one such visit in 1961, a member of Parliament sitting in front of him whispered: "I understand the old man is losing it—they say he's a bit gaga." Then, from behind him,

They Meet Again

Although he was still a member of Parliament, Churchill's 1959 visit to Washington was strictly social. The 84-year-old statesman wanted to spend time with his old friend Ike while he was still able to travel.

the whisperer heard the familiar lisping drawl: "Yes, and they say the old man is going deaf, too!"

It was Churchill's attempt to counter rumors that he had become senile, but he could not deny the ravages of close to nine decades. He knew his only remaining public role was like that of a monarch—he was a symbol embodying freedom, and the courage to fight for it.

On April 12, the sixteenth anniversary of Roosevelt's death, Sir Winston had a final look at america while aboard Aristotle Onassis's yacht, *Christina.* Joining Churchill on board as it sailed past the Statue of Liberty were his old friend Bernard Baruch and U.S. Ambassador to the United Nations, Adlai Stevenson. While the evening dinner was in progress, a call from the White House came. Churchill, whose first conversation with a U.S. president was with William McKinley, now spoke with John F. Kennedy. The new president wanted Churchill to visit the White House and proposed sending a special plane to bring him.

But just at that point, Churchill learned by phone that Clementine had taken ill. He declined Kennedy's offer and rushed back to England. At the Pan American terminal of Kennedy Airport, a crowd of 300 cheered Churchill as he arrived for his flight. He looked around, slightly startled, his eyes in an unfocused daze and the few tufts of his white hair whipping in the wind. Then he lifted his hat. The simple gesture was completely Churchill, and the people behind the gate waved back their response. It was his last moment on American soil.

Two years later, President Kennedy proclaimed Churchill the first honorary citizen of the United States by Act of Congress. "By adding his name to the rolls," said the president, "we mean to honor him—but his acceptance honors us far more, for no statement nor proclamation can enrich his name now—the name of Sir Winston Churchill is already legend."

Churchill, in a letter, generously accepted the honor and sent his son Randolph to stand in for him at the ceremonies. At the White House, Randolph read his father's valedictory: "I reject the view that Britain and the Commonwealth should now be relegated to a tame and minor role in the world."

It was the parting roar of the old Empire lion.

Just before adjournment of the House of Commons in 1964, Churchill made his last visit there, on July 27. Two fellow members helped him into the chamber and supported him when he made the customary bow of recognition to the speaker. He smiled and nodded and took his place on the front bench. He had not come to speak but to say good-bye. Former prime minister Harold Macmillan said what was in everyone's heart: "The life of the man we are today honoring is unique. The oldest

High Honor
On April 10, 1963, Churchill became the first honorary citizen of the United States. His special black passport contained a citizenship proclamation handwritten and signed by President Kennedy.

can recall nothing to compare with it, and the younger ones among you, however long you live, will never see the like again."

The next month, a stroke hospitalized him. Sir Winston was visited at Edward VII Hospital by Eisenhower; the former president had been in Europe for the twentieth anniversary of D day. When Eisenhower entered Churchill's hospital suite, his old friend's eyes lit up in recognition. Churchill was paralyzed and could not speak, but he put his right hand on the bedside table next to him. Eisenhower could see that Churchill was a dying man. His sagging body was propped up against the back of the bed, and his face flaccid.

On the bedside table, Churchill's small pink hand reached out for Eisenhower's. No words were uttered—the two men silently relived the battles they together fought for the ideals they mutually cherished. No words could have been more eloquent and poignant than the mute handclasp between two nations, two leaders, and two friends.

After nine minutes, Churchill unclasped his hand and slowly waved it in a V sign. Eisenhower went to the door. He said to the British aide who had accompanied him: "I just said good-bye to Winston, but you never say farewell to courage."

Last Birthday
Still in his trademark bow tie, Churchill greeted photographers at the window of his Hyde Park Gate home on his 90th (and final) birthday in 1964. To his right are Clementine and his nurse. Churchill celebrated with cake, a glass of champagne, and a few puffs of a cigar.

"The world does not end with the life of any man."

WINSTON CHURCHILL

After Churchill returned to his home at 28 Hyde Park Gate in September, it was a gentle decline for the venerable warrior. On November 30, he celebrated his ninetieth birthday. Clementine gave him a small golden heart engraved with the figure 90. Before lunch, Lady Churchill gathered the nursing staff in his bedroom for a glass of champagne. After lunch, he appeared for a photographer in the window of his town house. He was a slumped and feeble figure in a chair, with his limp hand raised in a V salute. Among the 70,000 greetings was a letter from Eisenhower:

"On this your Ninetieth Anniversary, I take particular pleasure in sending you felicitations. Our long and warm friendship is a source of great pride to

ST. PAUL'S CATHEDRAL

The great London fire of 1666 destroyed the original, Gothic cathedral of St. Paul's. For its replacement, architect Wren drew on the neoclassical style of the Louvre in Paris, as well as the baroque design of St. Peter's Basilica in Rome.

Seven months of bombing during the Blitz turned much of London into rubble and ashes, but Hitler's Luftwaffe never managed to hit St. Paul's Cathedral. It wasn't for lack of trying: All around the church, buildings were leveled, yet the great domed masterpiece remained. As much as Churchill himself, St. Paul's became a symbol of Britain's indomitable spirit.

St. Paul's was designed by England's greatest architect, Christopher Wren, who is buried there with the inscription, "If you seek my monument, look around you." When the cathedral was completed in 1681, King James II told Wren, "I find this cathedral awful, artificial and amusing." Churchill used these same words in lauding a building reputed to be Wren's at William and Mary College in Virginia—pointing out that in the 17th century, *awful* meant *awesome, artificial* meant *made artistically,* and *amusing* meant *amazing.* The awesome dome of St. Paul's inspired the U.S. Capitol.

Churchill chose St. Paul's for his state funeral, in a plan he dubbed "Operation Hope Not." As a closing hymn, he requested his favorite religious anthem, "The Battle Hymn of the Republic," which his American mother had taught him.

me, and I only wish that occasionally we could again have the opportunity to visit together.

"Mamie joins me in these sentiments and in sending to Clementine our affectionate greetings.

"Happy Birthday and may the years to come be filled with all good things. —Ike"

The family members who gathered at Churchill's London house knew it would be the final birthday celebration. In early December, he made his last public appearance at the Other Club. He sat at his usual place in the middle of the table beneath the windows that looked out at the Thames River. He said nothing but waved feebly to acknowledge greetings to him.

On Saturday evening, January 9, 1965, an ailing Sir Winston declined his nightly ritual of cigars and brandy. He said to his family: "It has been a grand journey—well worth making…[and then he paused for several seconds]… once." The sleep that evening turned into a coma from which he never awoke. Nine days later, a London *Times* editorial commented on the effect of his latest stroke: "Life is clearly ebbing away, but how long it will be until the crossing of the bar it is impossible to say."

Yet one person knew—Churchill himself. Long before, he had predicted to Jock Colville that he would die on January 24—the same day his father Randolph had died. Randolph passed at eight o'clock in the morning, and so did Winston, on Sunday, January 24, 1965. The old soldier who, in the previous century, had narrowly escaped being killed on four different continents died in his own bed.

The final tribute to Churchill, at St. Paul's Cathedral on January 30, was not so much a funeral as a festival celebrating the greatness of one man. Overhead, Hurricane and Spitfire planes flew in a V formation piloted by those who, twenty-five years before, had won the Battle of Britain. Inside, Queen Elizabeth seated Eisenhower next to attending heads of state including French President De Gaulle, King Olaf of Norway, King Baudouin of Belgium and Queen Juliana of the Netherlands—all of whom represented countries whose freedom had been redeemed by Churchill. The world leaders were not bowed in grief, but stood straight in proud salute to the memory of a man. If men wept, it was for the passing of an age where one man by himself could rouse the Free World.

A Nation Mourns
Clementine, in heavy veil, arrives at St. Paul's for her husband's state funeral—the first for a commoner since the Duke of Wellington's in 1852. Behind her are daughters Mary (left) and Sarah. Earlier, in Westminster Hall, 300,000 people waited in line to view Churchill's coffin.

Photo Credits

Page #/ Position	Credit	Page #/ Position	Credit	Page #/ Position	Credit
1-3	AP Wide World Photos	62	George Skadding/TimePix	119	Lofman/Pix Inc./TimePix
4-6	Hulton Archive/Getty Images	63-64	Hulton Archive/Getty Images	120-123	AP Wide World Photo
7	AP Wide World Photo	65	Eyewire/Getty Images	124	Mark Kauffman/TimePix
8-9	Joe Schilling/TimePix	66-67	AP Wide World Photo	125	Swim Ink/Corbis
10	AP Wide World Photo	68	Walter B. Lane/TimePix	126	Ralph Morse/TimePix
11	Mansell/TimePix	69	Photos12.com-Oasis	127	AP Wide World Photo
12	March of Time/TimePix	70	Hulton Archive/Getty Images	128	Ian Smith/TimePix
13	AP Wide World Photo	71	Frank Scherschel/TimePix	129-133	Hulton Archive/Getty Images
14	Mansell/TimePix	72	O. Hoppe /Mansell/TimePix	134	AP Wide World Photo
16-17	Brian Seed/TimePix	73	William C. Shrout/TimePix	135	Hulton Archive/Getty Images
17	DK Picture Library	74	Hulton Archive/Getty Images	136	Mark Kauffman/TimePix
18	Mansell/TimePix	75-76	AP Wide World Photo	137	AP Wide World Photo
19	Bettmann/Corbis	77	Heinrich Hoffmann/TimePix	138	Brian Seed/TimePix
20-22	TimePix	78-82	AP Wide World Photo	139	Hulton Archive/Getty Images
23	Hulton-Deutsch Collection/Corbis	83	Life Magazine Copyright Time Inc./TimePix	140	"The Lion and the Mouse" (oil on canvas) by Rubens, P.P.(1577-1640) and Snyders, F.(1579-1657) By Kind Permission of The Trustees of the Chequers Estate/The Bridgeman Art Library
24	AP Wide World Photo	84	AP Wide World Photo		
25	The Granger Collection	86	Hulton Archive/Getty Images		
27	AP Wide World Photo	87-91	AP Wide World Photo		
28	Mansell/TimePix	92	Hulton Archive/Getty Images		
29	Hulton Archive/Getty Images	93	Thomas D. McAvoy/TimePix		
30	Mansell/TimePix	94	AP Wide World Photo		
31-34	Hulton Archive/Getty Images	95	Hulton Archive/TimePix	141	Hulton Archive/Getty Images
35-36	TimePix	96-97	Department of Defense (DOD)/TimePix	142	Time Magazine Copyright Time Inc./TimePix
37	Hulton Archive/Getty Images				
38	Mansell/TimePix	98-99	Hulton Archive/Getty Images	143	Hulton Archive/Getty Images
38-39	Hulton Archive/Getty Images	100-102	AP Wide World Photo	144-145	AP Wide World Photo
40	DK Picture Library	103	Hulton Archive/Getty Images	146	Hulton Archive/Getty Images
41	Photos12.com	104	British Official/War Department/National Archives/TimePix	147-149	AP Wide World Photo
42-43	Hulton Archive/Getty Images			150	DK Picture Library
44-46	AP Wide World Photo			151	AP Wide World Photo
47	Mansell/TimePix	105	TimePix	159	© Bachrach
48-49	Hulton Archive/Getty Images	106	Leo Rosenthal/Pix Inc/TimePix	160	Hulton Archive/Getty Images
50	AP Wide World Photo				
51	Pictures Inc./TimePix	107	AP Wide World Photo		
52-55	Hulton Archive/Getty Images	108	Ed Clark/TimePix		
56-57	Underwood & Underwood/TimePix	109	AP Wide World Photo		
58	Pictures Inc./TimePix	111-112	Hulton Archive/Getty Images		
59	AP Wide World Photo	113	AP Wide World Photo		
60	Buyenlarge/TimePix	114-115	AP Wide World Photo		
61	Hulton Archive/Getty Images	116	Hulton Archive/Getty Images		
		117	AP Wide World Photo		

Jacket images:

Front:	Bettmann/Corbis
(left to right):	
1-2	Mansell/TimePix
3	AP Wide World Photo
4	Oswald Wild/TimePix
Author photo	© Bachrach

Acknowledgements

The publishers would like to thank A&E Networks, Avalon Publishing Group, and their associates for their hard work and good humor throughout this project. Special thanks go to Max Alexander, Tracy Armstead, and Lisa Vaughn for efforts above and beyond the call of duty, and to Sean Moore, f-stop Fitzgerald, and Will Balliett for their vision in conceiving this series and their determination to make it a reality. We would also like to extend our continued appreciation to ColourScan Ltd., Singapore, for their excellent work.

Avalon Publishing Group would like to thank Judith McQuown, Jonathan Gregg, and Nanette Cardon for their efforts on this project, as well as the kind cooperation of Hilary Johnston at TimePix, Yvette Reyes at AP Wide World Photo, Colombe Meurin at Photos12.com, and Valerie Zars at Hulton Getty. At DK, Chuck Lang for his support; Chuck Wills for his dogged pursuit of accuracy and good writing; Dirk Kaufman for his great design eye and Gregor Hall for keeping things moving with patience and understanding.

At AETN, Juan Davila, Chey Blake, Charles Wright, Liz Durkin and David Walmsley all helped put the pieces together, Cindy Berenson kept the ball rolling with her grateful professionalism and, most of all, thanks to Carrie Trimmer, who has supported this series and has contributed to it in so many ways above and beyond the call.

Additional Captions

pg. 8-9: Blenheim Palace.

pg. 20-21: Churchill as a young cavalry officer in India.

pg. 32-33: Parliament Square, London, around 1900.

pg. 44-45: British soldiers go "over the top" during the bloody trench warfare of World War I.

pg. 56-57: Hammersmith Broadway, London, during the General Strike of 1926.

pg. 66-67: Prime Minister Neville Chamberlain waves his peace accord with Hitler after returning from Munich in 1938.

pg. 80-81: Troops of the British Expeditionary Force view the Nazi bombardment of Dunkirk after being evacuated from the beach.

pg. 98-99: St. Paul's Cathedral stands tall during the devastating London Blitz.

pg. 114-115: Churchill campaigning in 1951, from the roof of the Red Lion Hotel in High Wycombe.

pg. 132-133: Churchill leaving 10 Downing Street on April 5, 1955, to offer his resignation to Queen Elizabeth.

pg. 144-145: Churchill's coffin leaves Westminster Hall for the funeral at St. Paul's Cathedral on January 30, 1965.

Index

Author's Acknowledgements

First I want to thank my mother. She would wake me up from my nap and make me listen to Winston Churchill in radio broadcasts in 1940. My first long pair of trousers was a miniature R.A.F. uniform. It was adorned with R.A.F. wings, which had been awarded to my mother for her work with "Bundles for Britain."

My mother also insisted that I accept an English-Speaking Union Scholarship to Britain. That year (1952-53) in Britain when I attended Stowe School, shaped my life. I met Winston Churchill and danced with the Queen. The English-Speaking Union (E.S.U.) was responsible for that year, and also made it possible for me to attend the Commonwealth Parliamentary luncheon on May 29, 1953. There I was introduced to Prime Minister Winston Churchill, who told me: "Young man, study history, study history. In history lies all the secrets of state craft." I would see Churchill three times more—twice in the House of Commons and once in Washington D.C. in 1959. While at Stowe on Christmas holiday, I stayed at the home of the Second Earl of Balfour, where I stayed in the room and study of the late first earl, Arthur Balfour—the prime minister and foreign secretary, who remained a friend of Churchill's until he died in 1930.

A fellow "Old Stoic" I first met when at the school was Anthony Montague-Brown, who for years was private parliamentary secretary to Winston Churchill. In 1966, at a dinner honoring Churchill, he introduced me to Lady Churchill, who had been recently made Baroness Spencer-Churchill.

In 1963, 1966, and 1986, I went on speaking tours in Britain organized by the E.S.U. During those visits, I met many colleagues and friends, as well as members of Churchill's family.

I dined with Randolph Churchill at the Conservative Party Conference in 1963. Over the years, I have kept up my friendship with his son, Winston Churchill. I have been Winston's guest several times at the House of Commons dining room, as well as at his house. I also treasure my friendship with Edwina Sandys, the New York sculptress, who is also Churchill's grandchild.

My wife and I were also houseguests of the Earl and Countess of Avon (Anthony Eden), who served as foreign secretary under Churchill and succeeded him as prime minister. Lady Avon was the former Clarissa Churchill, a niece of Winston.

Her brother, John Spencer Churchill, was my houseguest in Washington in 1970, when I was working in the Nixon White House. I was introduced to John Churchill by the late Kay Halle, a longtime

Churchill's Study at Chartwell

friend of the Churchill family, who was mainly responsible for the honorary U.S. citizenship conferred on Churchill in 1963.

Through Kay Halle, I met Grace Hamblin, the longtime secretary to Churchill. Twice I have visited Grace at her home at Westerham, Kent (near Chartwell). Outside her cottage stands a statue of Churchill.

My wife and I also count as a dear friend Jamie Crathorne for about forty years. Lord Crathorne's father, then Sir Thomas Dugdale, served in the cabinet during Churchill's second tenure at 10 Downing Street and later as chairman of the Conservative Party. In the abdication crisis, he was the parliamentary secretary to Prime Minister Stanley Baldwin. Sir Thomas' wife, Lady Crathorne, was the sister of Lady Asquith, wife of Prime Minister Herbert Asquith. I stayed with them at Crathorne Hall on several occasions. Jamie's godfather was Lord Mountbatten.

I also want to thank Lord Cope, now spokesman for the Conservative Party in the House of Lords. John Cope served in the cabinet of both Prime Ministers Margaret Thatcher and John Major.

I met John Cope at the house of Sir Cyril Osborne, Member of Parliament, where I was a guest in 1963. A Conservative, he served with Churchill in Parliament from after the war to 1964. Sir Cyril's daughter, Hazel, now Baroness Byford, and her husband, Commander Byford, are the oldest of friends. I attended her investiture in the House of Lords in 1999. She is now agricultural spokesperson for the Conservative Party in the House of Lords.

Another Churchill appointee who reminisced with me about the prime minister was Sir Alec Douglas-Home. He was parliamentary secretary of state for Scotland in the Churchill government and earlier parliamentary secretary to Prime Minister Neville Chamberlain. He was later prime minister in 1963 and in 1973 foreign secretary under Edward Heath. (Home was the chief of my family clan of Humes.)

I am grateful to Sir Martin Gilbert, the preeminent Churchill historian, and Richard Langforth, head of the International Churchill Society. I also am thankful to former Prime Minister Heath, who hosted me and my friend Dr. Jarvis Ryals in 1999. Without Dr. Jarvis and Mary Jo Ryals, who endowed my professorship at the University of Southern Colorado, this book may have not been possible.

I also had dinner twice with former Prime Minister Harold Macmillan— once at the Beefsteak Club in 1966 and then at the Woodrow Wilson Center at the Smithsonian in 1982.

At the University, I have had the assistance of one of my oldest friends, Professor Dick Eisenbeis, as well as Professor Lia Sissom, and Carol Toponce.

My typist, Linda Graham, was a superb professional, who met a severe deadline.

Finally, my wife, Dianne, of 45 years, who surpasses Lady Churchill in handling her demanding husband.

—James C. Humes